SRA
Connecting
Math Concepts

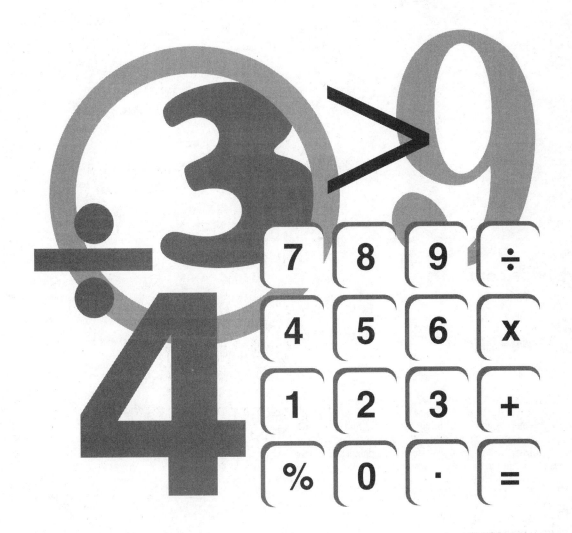

Columbus, Ohio

The McGraw-Hill Companies

www.sra4kids.com

Send all inquiries to:
SRA/McGraw-Hill
8787 Orion Place
Columbus, OH 43240-4027

Printed in the United States of America.

ISBN 0-02-684657-8

1 2 3 4 5 6 7 8 9 0 POH 06 05 04 03 02

Lesson 1

Part 1

a. **413**
How many digits? _____
How many hundreds? _____
How many tens? _____
How many ones? _____

b. **40**
How many digits? _____
How many tens? _____
How many ones? _____

c. **509**
How many digits? _____
How many tens? _____
How many ones? _____

d. **6**
How many digits? _____
How many ones? _____

Part 2

a. $4 + 10 =$ _____ $4 + 9 =$ _____

b. $6 + 10 =$ _____ $6 + 9 =$ _____

c. $3 + 10 =$ _____ $3 + 9 =$ _____

d. $8 + 10 =$ _____ $8 + 9 =$ _____

e. $2 + 10 =$ _____ $2 + 9 =$ _____

Part 3

a. $+$ $9 \xrightarrow{} 11 \rightarrow \square$

b. _____ $\square \xrightarrow{} 9 \rightarrow 15$

c. _____ $2 \xrightarrow{} 6 \rightarrow \square$

d. _____ $3 \xrightarrow{} 19 \rightarrow \square$

e. _____ $9 \xrightarrow{\square} 21$

f. _____ $\square \xrightarrow{8} 14$

g. _____ $15 \xrightarrow{} 31 \rightarrow \square$

Part 4

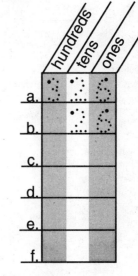

1

a. $\begin{array}{r} 52 \\ +20 \\ \hline \end{array}$ b. $\begin{array}{r} 13 \\ 61 \\ +21 \\ \hline \end{array}$ c. $\begin{array}{r} 12 \\ 22 \\ +22 \\ \hline \end{array}$ d. $\begin{array}{r} 630 \\ 120 \\ +216 \\ \hline \end{array}$ e. $\begin{array}{r} 422 \\ 200 \\ +214 \\ \hline \end{array}$ f. $\begin{array}{r} 121 \\ 541 \\ +217 \\ \hline \end{array}$ g. $\begin{array}{r} 523 \\ 30 \\ +122 \\ \hline \end{array}$

Part 6   **Independent Work**

a. $\begin{array}{r} 7 \\ -0 \\ \hline \end{array}$ b. $\begin{array}{r} 8 \\ -1 \\ \hline \end{array}$ c. $\begin{array}{r} 10 \\ -1 \\ \hline \end{array}$ d. $\begin{array}{r} 4 \\ -4 \\ \hline \end{array}$ e. $\begin{array}{r} 6 \\ -5 \\ \hline \end{array}$ f. $\begin{array}{r} 6 \\ -1 \\ \hline \end{array}$ g. $\begin{array}{r} 6 \\ -0 \\ \hline \end{array}$ h. $\begin{array}{r} 6 \\ -6 \\ \hline \end{array}$ i. $\begin{array}{r} 5 \\ -5 \\ \hline \end{array}$

j. $\begin{array}{r} 5 \\ -4 \\ \hline \end{array}$ k. $\begin{array}{r} 5 \\ -1 \\ \hline \end{array}$ l. $\begin{array}{r} 5 \\ -0 \\ \hline \end{array}$ m. $\begin{array}{r} 3 \\ -2 \\ \hline \end{array}$ n. $\begin{array}{r} 7 \\ -6 \\ \hline \end{array}$ o. $\begin{array}{r} 8 \\ -7 \\ \hline \end{array}$ p. $\begin{array}{r} 9 \\ -1 \\ \hline \end{array}$ q. $\begin{array}{r} 9 \\ -9 \\ \hline \end{array}$ r. $\begin{array}{r} 3 \\ -0 \\ \hline \end{array}$

Part 7

a. $9 + 1 =$ ____ b. $5 + 1 =$ ____ c. $7 + 1 =$ ____ d. $10 + 1 =$ ____

$9 + 2 =$ ____ $5 + 2 =$ ____ $7 + 2 =$ ____ $10 + 2 =$ ____

$9 + 3 =$ ____ $5 + 3 =$ ____ $7 + 3 =$ ____ $10 + 3 =$ ____

Lesson 2

a. 960
How many digits? _____
How many hundreds? _____
How many ones? _____

d. 610
How many digits? _____
How many hundreds? _____
How many ones? _____

b. 405
How many digits? _____
How many tens? _____
How many ones? _____

e. 73
How many digits? _____
How many tens? _____
How many ones? _____

c. 2
How many digits? _____
How many ones? _____

f. 50
How many digits? _____
How many tens? _____
How many ones? _____

Part 2

a. _____
b. _____
c. _____
d. _____
e. _____
f. _____
g. _____
h. _____

$23 \quad \boxed{} \rightarrow 50$

$4 \quad 27 \rightarrow \boxed{}$

$2 \quad 6 \rightarrow \boxed{}$

$\boxed{} \quad 5 \rightarrow 6$

$185 \quad 37 \rightarrow \boxed{}$

$\boxed{} \quad 8 \rightarrow 10$

$18 \quad 7 \rightarrow \boxed{}$

$2 \quad \boxed{} \rightarrow 12$

Part 3

a. $\underline{1 \qquad 5} \rightarrow$ _____

b. $\underline{2 \qquad 7} \rightarrow$ _____

c. $\underline{1 \qquad 6} \rightarrow$ _____

d. $\underline{1 \qquad 2} \rightarrow$ _____

e. $\underline{2 \qquad 8} \rightarrow$ _____

f. $\underline{2 \qquad 2} \rightarrow$ _____

g. $\underline{2 \qquad 5} \rightarrow$ _____

h. $\underline{1 \qquad 10} \rightarrow$ _____

i. $\underline{2 \qquad 10} \rightarrow$ _____

j. $\underline{2 \qquad 9} \rightarrow$ _____

Part 4

a. 10 + 3 = ___   9 + 3 = ___

b. 10 + 7 = ___   9 + 7 = ___

c. 10 + 5 = ___   9 + 5 = ___

d. 6 + 10 = ___   6 + 9 = ___

e. 2 + 10 = ___   2 + 9 = ___

f. 8 + 10 = ___   8 + 9 = ___

Part 5

a.
```
  521
   25
+221
```

b.
```
  123
  110
+702
```

c.
```
  503
  200
+ 41
```

d.
```
  210
  462
+226
```

e.
```
   11
   81
+ 25
```

f.
```
   10
   75
+ 21
```

Part 6

a. 5 hundreds
   +
   6 tens
   +
   2 ones
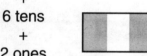

b. 1 ten
   +
   2 ones

c. 7 hundreds
   +
   no tens
   +
   no ones
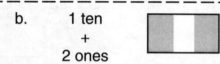

d. 2 tens
   +
   no ones

e. 1 ten
   +
   7 ones

f. 3 hundreds
   +
   no tens
   +
   2 ones

g. 4 tens
   +
   1 one

h. 1 ten
   +
   4 ones

Part 7   Independent Work

a.
```
  7
 −7
```

b.
```
  9
 −9
```

c.
```
  3
 −3
```

d.
```
  3
 −2
```

e.
```
  3
 −1
```

f.
```
  3
 −0
```

g.
```
 10
 − 0
```

h.
```
 10
 − 1
```

i.
```
 10
 −10
```

j.
```
  5
 −4
```

k.
```
  7
 −6
```

l.
```
  7
 −1
```

Lesson 3

Part 1

a.
$$\begin{array}{r} 3 \\ +9 \\ \hline \end{array}$$
b.
$$\begin{array}{r} 5 \\ +9 \\ \hline \end{array}$$
c.
$$\begin{array}{r} 8 \\ +9 \\ \hline \end{array}$$
d.
$$\begin{array}{r} 9 \\ +4 \\ \hline \end{array}$$
e.
$$\begin{array}{r} 9 \\ +6 \\ \hline \end{array}$$
f.
$$\begin{array}{r} 9 \\ +2 \\ \hline \end{array}$$
g.
$$\begin{array}{r} 9 \\ +7 \\ \hline \end{array}$$

Part 2

a. □ →4→ 5

b. □ →9→ 17

c. 8 →9→ □

d. □ →14→ 28

e. 12 →16→ □

f. 2 →3→ □

g. □ →4→ 6

h. □ →3→ 18

i. 1 →7→ □

Part 3

a.
$$\begin{array}{r} 19 \\ +\ 3 \\ \hline \end{array}$$
b.
$$\begin{array}{r} 36 \\ +29 \\ \hline \end{array}$$

c.
$$\begin{array}{r} 32 \\ +28 \\ \hline \end{array}$$
d.
$$\begin{array}{r} 29 \\ +91 \\ \hline \end{array}$$

e.
$$\begin{array}{r} 39 \\ +98 \\ \hline \end{array}$$
f.
$$\begin{array}{r} 47 \\ +29 \\ \hline \end{array}$$

Part 4

a. 2 →7→ __
b. 1 →7→ __
c. 2 →10→ __
d. 1 →1→ __

e. 1 →3→ __
f. 1 →10→ __
g. 2 →4→ __
h. 1 →6→ __

i. 2 →8→ __
j. 1 →4→ __
k. 2 →9→ __
l. 1 →5→ __

m. 2 →5→ __

5

A	
B	

Part 6

Independent Work

a.	b.	c.	d.	e.	f.
305	735	789	365	111	126
202	21	110	222	246	300
+111	+ 2	+100	+102	+ 20	+ 42

Part 7

a.	b.	c.	d.	e.	f.	g.	h.	i.
4	4	4	4	4	8	8	6	6
−1	−2	−3	−0	−4	−1	−2	−1	−2

Part 8 Write the numerals.

a.   5 hundreds
+
no tens
+
2 ones

c.   4 hundreds
+
no tens
+
no ones

b.   3 hundreds
+
6 tens
+
no ones

d.   5 tens
+
no ones

e.   1 ten
+
2 ones

Lesson 4

a. 4   10 ⟶ __

b. 6   9 ⟶ __

c. 8   9 ⟶ __

d. 2   10 ⟶ __

e. 3   9 ⟶ __

f. 8   10 ⟶ __

g. 5   9 ⟶ __

h. 5   10 ⟶ __

i. 9   9 ⟶ __

j. 2   9 ⟶ __

k. 1   10 ⟶ __

l. 10   10 ⟶ __

m. 9   10 ⟶ __

Part 2

a. 56   b. 84   c. 376   d. 24   e. 79   f. 694   g. 385
   −11   −21   −106   −13   −18   −590   −370

Part 3

a. 39   b. 12   c. 14   d. 64   e. 49   f. 89
   +95   +87   +79   +22   +21   +96

Part 4

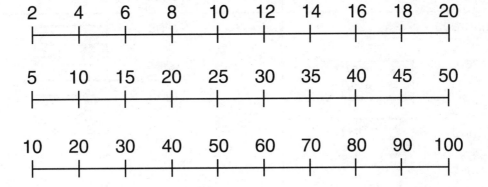

a. 2 x 3 = ____   b. 5 x 3 = ____   c. 10 x 3 = ____

d. 5 x 6 = ____   e. 10 x 4 = ____   f. 2 x 7 = ____

7

a. ☐ →11→ 20

b. 20 →11→ ☐

c. 2 →7→ ☐

d. ☐ →7→ 8

e. ☐ →51→ 76

f. 12 →19→ ☐

_____

_____

_____

_____

_____

_____

Part 6   Independent Work

a. 8	b. 8	c. 8	d. 5
−0	−1	−2	−0

e. 5	f. 5	g. 9	h. 9
−1	−2	−0	−1

i. 9	j. 5	k. 5	l. 6
−2	−1	−2	−1

Part 7

a. 6	b. 6	c. 6	d. 9	e. 9	f. 9	g. 8	h. 8	i. 6
−6	−5	−4	−9	−8	−7	−8	−7	−6

Part 8   Write the numerals.

a. 3 hundreds
    +
    9 tens
    +
    6 ones

b. 7 hundreds
    +
    no tens
    +
    9 ones

c. 6 tens
    +
    5 ones

d. 8 hundreds
    +
    no tens
    +
    6 ones

e. 4 tens
    +
    2 ones

f. 5 tens
    +
    no ones

Lesson 5

Part 1

a. 309	b. 264	c. 122	d. 321	e. 590	f. 321
+124	+192	+487	+578	+296	+ 88

Part 2

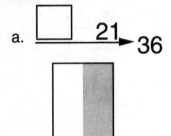

a.

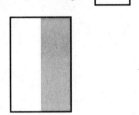

b.

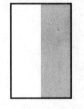

c.

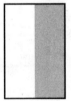

d. 12 63 →

e. 64 → 85

Part 3

a.	b.	c.	d.	e.	f.
+	+	+	+	+	+
8 7	3 6	7 3	5 4	2 7	6 1

Part 4

a. 547	b. 45	c. 395	d. 546	e. 419	f. 765
− 36	−10	− 14	−232	−208	−160

9

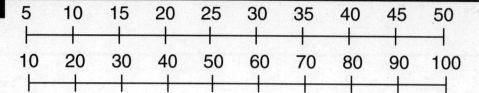

| 5 | 10 | 15 | 20 | 25 | 30 | 35 | 40 | 45 | 50 |

| 10 | 20 | 30 | 40 | 50 | 60 | 70 | 80 | 90 | 100 |

Part 6

a. $10 \times 8 =$ _____   b. $5 \times 4 =$ _____   c. $10 \times 4 =$ _____

d. $5 \times 6 =$ _____   e. $10 \times 2 =$ _____   f. $5 \times 8 =$ _____

Part 7

9
1__
2__
3__
4__
5__
6__
7__
8__
9__

a. $\begin{array}{r} 6 \\ -1 \\ \hline \end{array}$ b. $\begin{array}{r} 6 \\ -2 \\ \hline \end{array}$ c. $\begin{array}{r} 8 \\ -1 \\ \hline \end{array}$ d. $\begin{array}{r} 8 \\ -2 \\ \hline \end{array}$ e. $\begin{array}{r} 9 \\ -0 \\ \hline \end{array}$ f. $\begin{array}{r} 9 \\ -2 \\ \hline \end{array}$

g. $\begin{array}{r} 5 \\ -1 \\ \hline \end{array}$ h. $\begin{array}{r} 5 \\ -2 \\ \hline \end{array}$ i. $\begin{array}{r} 6 \\ -5 \\ \hline \end{array}$ j. $\begin{array}{r} 6 \\ -4 \\ \hline \end{array}$ k. $\begin{array}{r} 8 \\ -7 \\ \hline \end{array}$ l. $\begin{array}{r} 8 \\ -6 \\ \hline \end{array}$

m. $\begin{array}{r} 9 \\ -1 \\ \hline \end{array}$ n. $\begin{array}{r} 9 \\ -8 \\ \hline \end{array}$ o. $\begin{array}{r} 5 \\ -4 \\ \hline \end{array}$ p. $\begin{array}{r} 5 \\ -3 \\ \hline \end{array}$ q. $\begin{array}{r} 5 \\ -2 \\ \hline \end{array}$ r. $\begin{array}{r} 6 \\ -2 \\ \hline \end{array}$

Part 8 Write the numerals.

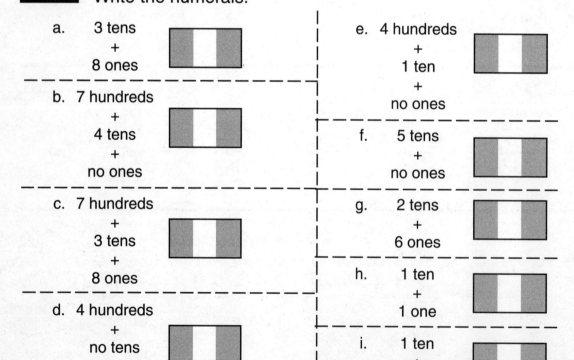

a. 3 tens
    +
    8 ones

b. 7 hundreds
    +
    4 tens
    +
    no ones

c. 7 hundreds
    +
    3 tens
    +
    8 ones

d. 4 hundreds
    +
    no tens
    +
    1 one

e. 4 hundreds
    +
    1 ten
    +
    no ones

f. 5 tens
    +
    no ones

g. 2 tens
    +
    6 ones

h. 1 ten
    +
    1 one

i. 1 ten
    +
    5 ones

Lesson 6

Part 1

a. $16 - 10 =$ ____ $16 - 9 =$ ____

b. $13 - 10 =$ ____ $13 - 9 =$ ____

c. $18 - 10 =$ ____ $18 - 9 =$ ____

d. $12 - 10 =$ ____ $12 - 9 =$ ____

e. $17 - 10 =$ ____ $17 - 9 =$ ____

Part 2

a.
```
   +
    7 1
```

b.
```
   +
    2 3
```

c.
```
   +
    9 5
```

d.
```
   +
    6 1
```

e.
```
   +
    1 6
```

f.
```
   +
    4 8
```

Part 3

a. $9 \times 2 =$ ____   b. $10 \times 4 =$ ____   c. $9 \times 4 =$ ____

d. $5 \times 4 =$ ____   e. $10 \times 3 =$ ____   f. $5 \times 2 =$ ____

Part 4

a.
```
  1 8 9
 +1 3 3
```

b.
```
    4 2
 +2 9 8
```

c.
```
  3 7 0
 +2 9 8
```

d.
```
  6 0 9
 +2 0 9
```

e.
```
  6 8 5
 + 9 9
```

f.
```
  3 5 6
 +2 9 2
```

Part 5

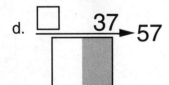

a. ☐ → 27 → 49

b. 27 → 40 → ☐

c. 32 → 37 → ☐

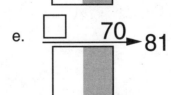

d. ☐ → 37 → 57

e. ☐ → 70 → 81

	A	
	B	

a. $10 + 4 =$ _____   b. $10 + 7 =$ _____   c. $9 + 5 =$ _____

d. $9 + 7 =$ _____   e. $9 + 3 =$ _____   f. $10 + 3 =$ _____

g. $9 + 9 =$ _____   h. $2 + 9 =$ _____   i. $5 + 9 =$ _____

j. $8 + 9 =$ _____   k. $2 + 10 =$ _____   l. $7 + 10 =$ _____

m. $6 + 9 =$ _____   n. $10 + 9 =$ _____

Part 7   Independent Work

a. $\begin{array}{r} 439 \\ -321 \\ \hline \end{array}$ b. $\begin{array}{r} 798 \\ -691 \\ \hline \end{array}$ c. $\begin{array}{r} 875 \\ -222 \\ \hline \end{array}$ d. $\begin{array}{r} 753 \\ -250 \\ \hline \end{array}$ e. $\begin{array}{r} 775 \\ -102 \\ \hline \end{array}$ f. $\begin{array}{r} 657 \\ -507 \\ \hline \end{array}$

Part 8

a. $\begin{array}{r} 8 \\ -1 \\ \hline \end{array}$ b. $\begin{array}{r} 8 \\ -2 \\ \hline \end{array}$ c. $\begin{array}{r} 8 \\ -7 \\ \hline \end{array}$ d. $\begin{array}{r} 8 \\ -6 \\ \hline \end{array}$ e. $\begin{array}{r} 5 \\ -4 \\ \hline \end{array}$ f. $\begin{array}{r} 5 \\ -1 \\ \hline \end{array}$ g. $\begin{array}{r} 5 \\ -2 \\ \hline \end{array}$ h. $\begin{array}{r} 5 \\ -3 \\ \hline \end{array}$

i. $\begin{array}{r} 9 \\ -8 \\ \hline \end{array}$ j. $\begin{array}{r} 9 \\ -7 \\ \hline \end{array}$ k. $\begin{array}{r} 9 \\ -9 \\ \hline \end{array}$ l. $\begin{array}{r} 9 \\ -8 \\ \hline \end{array}$ m. $\begin{array}{r} 7 \\ -6 \\ \hline \end{array}$ n. $\begin{array}{r} 7 \\ -5 \\ \hline \end{array}$ o. $\begin{array}{r} 8 \\ -2 \\ \hline \end{array}$ p. $\begin{array}{r} 9 \\ -2 \\ \hline \end{array}$

q. $\begin{array}{r} 9 \\ -0 \\ \hline \end{array}$ r. $\begin{array}{r} 4 \\ -2 \\ \hline \end{array}$ s. $\begin{array}{r} 5 \\ -2 \\ \hline \end{array}$ t. $\begin{array}{r} 6 \\ -2 \\ \hline \end{array}$ u. $\begin{array}{r} 7 \\ -2 \\ \hline \end{array}$ v. $\begin{array}{r} 7 \\ -1 \\ \hline \end{array}$ w. $\begin{array}{r} 7 \\ -7 \\ \hline \end{array}$ x. $\begin{array}{r} 7 \\ -0 \\ \hline \end{array}$

Lesson 7

Part 1

a. 5 x 3 = ____   b. 9 x 3 = ____   c. 9 x 5 = ____

d. 5 x 5 = ____   e. 2 x 5 = ____   f. 10 x 5 = ____

Part 2

a. 13 − 10 = ___   13 − 9 = ___

b. 18 − 10 = ___   18 − 9 = ___

c. 15 − 10 = ___   15 − 9 = ___

d. 12 − 10 = ___   12 − 9 = ___

e. 17 − 10 = ___   17 − 9 = ___

Part 3

a. 56   b. 96   c. 84

d. 51   e. 45   f. 72

Part 4

a. 984   b. 776   c. 398
   −974   −765   − 81

d. 583   e. 307   f. 581
   −410   −107   −201

Part 5

a.
2   8 → __
3   8 → __

b.
2   5 → __
3   5 → __

c.
2   9 → __
3   9 → __

d.
2   7 → __
3   7 → __

e.
2   6 → __
3   6 → __

Part 6

a. ☐ —9→ 29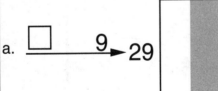

b. 72 —6→ ☐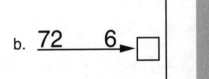

c. ☐ —23→ 55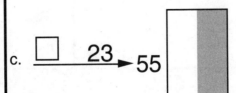

d. 40 —26→ ☐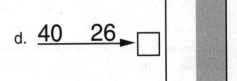

13

a. $\begin{array}{r}222\\+298\\\hline\end{array}$ b. $\begin{array}{r}90\\+596\\\hline\end{array}$ c. $\begin{array}{r}124\\+299\\\hline\end{array}$ d. $\begin{array}{r}375\\+292\\\hline\end{array}$

e. $\begin{array}{r}355\\+\ 99\\\hline\end{array}$ f. $\begin{array}{r}612\\+188\\\hline\end{array}$ g. $\begin{array}{r}378\\+221\\\hline\end{array}$ h. $\begin{array}{r}316\\+109\\\hline\end{array}$

Part 8 Independent Work

a. $\begin{array}{r}8\\-2\\\hline\end{array}$ b. $\begin{array}{r}9\\-2\\\hline\end{array}$ c. $\begin{array}{r}10\\-\ 2\\\hline\end{array}$ d. $\begin{array}{r}7\\-2\\\hline\end{array}$ e. $\begin{array}{r}6\\-2\\\hline\end{array}$ f. $\begin{array}{r}6\\-1\\\hline\end{array}$ g. $\begin{array}{r}6\\-0\\\hline\end{array}$ h. $\begin{array}{r}6\\-6\\\hline\end{array}$ i. $\begin{array}{r}6\\-5\\\hline\end{array}$

j. $\begin{array}{r}6\\-4\\\hline\end{array}$ k. $\begin{array}{r}7\\-5\\\hline\end{array}$ l. $\begin{array}{r}7\\-6\\\hline\end{array}$ m. $\begin{array}{r}7\\-7\\\hline\end{array}$ n. $\begin{array}{r}5\\-3\\\hline\end{array}$ o. $\begin{array}{r}5\\-4\\\hline\end{array}$ p. $\begin{array}{r}5\\-5\\\hline\end{array}$ q. $\begin{array}{r}5\\-1\\\hline\end{array}$ r. $\begin{array}{r}5\\-2\\\hline\end{array}$

Lesson 8

Part 1

a. $1 + 1 =$ ____
b. $2 + 2 =$ ____
c. $3 + 3 =$ ____
d. $4 + 4 =$ ____
e. $5 + 5 =$ ____

f. $6 + 6 =$ ____
g. $7 + 7 =$ ____
h. $8 + 8 =$ ____
i. $9 + 9 =$ ____
j. $10 + 10 =$ ____

Part 2

a. $4 + 4 =$ ____
b. $7 + 7 =$ ____
c. $8 + 8 =$ ____
d. $3 + 3 =$ ____
e. $5 + 5 =$ ____
f. $6 + 6 =$ ____

Part 3

a. 31 b. 63 c. 45 d. 91 e. 23 f. 78

Part 4

a. □ —9→ 13

b. 3 —9→ □

c. □ —9→ 10

d. 4 —9→ □

e. 2 —9→ □

f. □ —9→ 12

g. 1 —9→ □

h. □ —9→ 11

Part 5

a. 2 —7→ ___
   3 —7→ ___

b. 2 —6→ ___
   3 —6→ ___

c. 2 —4→ ___
   3 —4→ ___

d. 2 —9→ ___
   3 —9→ ___

e. 2 —8→ ___
   3 —8→ ___

Part 6

a. 9 x 6 = ____   b. 2 x 6 = ____   c. 5 x 6 = ____

d. 2 x 4 = ____   e. 5 x 4 = ____   f. 9 x 4 = ____

Part 7

a. 15   b. 17   c. 13   d. 16   e. 18   f. 11   g. 14   h. 12
  – 9   – 9   – 9   – 9   – 9   – 9   – 9   – 9

Part 8

a. □ —74→ 99

b. 35 —45→ □

c. □ —19→ 59

Part 9   Independent Work

a.   307
   – 101

b.   776
   – 765

c.   984
   –   72

d.   581
   – 201

Lesson 9

Part 1

a.
$$\begin{array}{r} 15 \\ -5 \\ \hline \end{array}$$

b.
$$\begin{array}{r} 15 \\ -6 \\ \hline \end{array}$$

c.
$$\begin{array}{r} 13 \\ -4 \\ \hline \end{array}$$

d.
$$\begin{array}{r} 17 \\ -7 \\ \hline \end{array}$$

e.
$$\begin{array}{r} 14 \\ -4 \\ \hline \end{array}$$

f.
$$\begin{array}{r} 14 \\ -5 \\ \hline \end{array}$$

g.
$$\begin{array}{r} 18 \\ -9 \\ \hline \end{array}$$

h.
$$\begin{array}{r} 16 \\ -6 \\ \hline \end{array}$$

i.
$$\begin{array}{r} 12 \\ -2 \\ \hline \end{array}$$

j.
$$\begin{array}{r} 17 \\ -8 \\ \hline \end{array}$$

k.
$$\begin{array}{r} 13 \\ -3 \\ \hline \end{array}$$

Part 2

a.
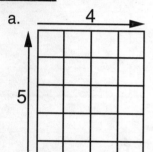

_____ squares

b.
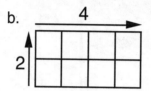

_____ squares

c.
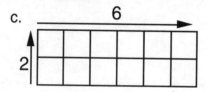

_____ squares

d.

_____ squares

Part 3

a.
$$\begin{array}{r} 53 \\ -19 \\ \hline \end{array}$$

b.
$$\begin{array}{r} 71 \\ -39 \\ \hline \end{array}$$

c.
$$\begin{array}{r} 90 \\ -21 \\ \hline \end{array}$$

d.
$$\begin{array}{r} 86 \\ -19 \\ \hline \end{array}$$

Part 4

a. $ 7.12

b. $ 9.03

c. $15.07

d. $ 2.30

e. $ 5.09

Part 5

a. _____

b. _____

c. _____

d. _____

e. _____

a. 3 → 6 → ___   e. 5 → 6 → ___   i. 4 → 6 → ___   _____

b. 4 → 6 → ___   f. 3 → 6 → ___   j. 6 → 6 → ___   _____

c. 5 → 6 → ___   g. 6 → 6 → ___   k. 3 → 6 → ___   _____

d. 6 → 6 → ___   h. 4 → 6 → ___   l. 5 → 6 → ___   _____

Part 7

a. $1 + 1 =$ ___   k. $6 + 6 =$ ___

b. $2 + 2 =$ ___   l. $9 + 9 =$ ___

c. $3 + 3 =$ ___   m. $5 + 5 =$ ___

d. $4 + 4 =$ ___   n. $3 + 3 =$ ___

e. $5 + 5 =$ ___   o. $8 + 8 =$ ___

f. $6 + 6 =$ ___   p. $10 + 10 =$ ___

g. $7 + 7 =$ ___   q. $2 + 2 =$ ___

h. $8 + 8 =$ ___   r. $4 + 4 =$ ___

i. $9 + 9 =$ ___   s. $1 + 1 =$ ___

j. $10 + 10 =$ ___   t. $7 + 7 =$ ___

Part 8

a. $5 \times 3 =$ ___

b. $5 \times 1 =$ ___

c. $2 \times 3 =$ ___

d. $2 \times 1 =$ ___

e. $9 \times 1 =$ ___

f. $9 \times 2 =$ ___

g. $9 \times 3 =$ ___

h. $2 \times 5 =$ ___

i. $2 \times 6 =$ ___

j. $2 \times 7 =$ ___

k. $10 \times 2 =$ ___

l. $10 \times 3 =$ ___

Part 9   **Independent Work**

a.
$$\begin{array}{r} 382 \\ +129 \\ \hline \end{array}$$

b.
$$\begin{array}{r} 209 \\ +647 \\ \hline \end{array}$$

c.
$$\begin{array}{r} 483 \\ +119 \\ \hline \end{array}$$

d.
$$\begin{array}{r} 492 \\ +208 \\ \hline \end{array}$$

Part 10

a. $3 + 4 =$ ___

b. $3 + 7 =$ ___

c. $3 + 6 =$ ___

d. $3 + 8 =$ ___

e. $3 + 7 =$ ___

Lesson 10

a. 3   6 ⟶ ___

b. 4   6 ⟶ ___

c. 5   6 ⟶ ___

d. 6   6 ⟶ ___

e. 5   6 ⟶ ___

f. 6   6 ⟶ ___

g. 3   6 ⟶ ___

h. 4   6 ⟶ ___

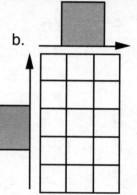

Part 2

a. 8 + 8 = _____

b. 2 + 2 = _____

c. 6 + 6 = _____

d. 4 + 4 = _____

e. 9 + 9 = _____

f. 10 + 10 = _____

g. 3 + 3 = _____

h. 5 + 5 = _____

i. 7 + 7 = _____

Part 3

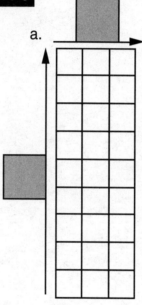

a.

_____squares

b.

_____squares

Part 4

a. 2   4 ⟶ 6

_____

_____

b. 4   6 ⟶ 10

_____

_____

c. 12   13 ⟶ 25

_____

_____

d. 5   6 ⟶ 11

_____

_____

Part 5

a. $\begin{array}{r} 17 \\ -\ 7 \\ \hline \end{array}$
b. $\begin{array}{r} 17 \\ -\ 8 \\ \hline \end{array}$
c. $\begin{array}{r} 13 \\ -\ 4 \\ \hline \end{array}$
d. $\begin{array}{r} 16 \\ -\ 7 \\ \hline \end{array}$
e. $\begin{array}{r} 15 \\ -\ 5 \\ \hline \end{array}$

f. $\begin{array}{r} 12 \\ -\ 3 \\ \hline \end{array}$
g. $\begin{array}{r} 19 \\ -\ 9 \\ \hline \end{array}$
h. $\begin{array}{r} 14 \\ -\ 5 \\ \hline \end{array}$
i. $\begin{array}{r} 14 \\ -\ 4 \\ \hline \end{array}$
j. $\begin{array}{r} 18 \\ -\ 9 \\ \hline \end{array}$

Part 6

a. $\begin{array}{r} 36 \\ -17 \\ \hline \end{array}$
b. $\begin{array}{r} 64 \\ -25 \\ \hline \end{array}$
c. $\begin{array}{r} 84 \\ -23 \\ \hline \end{array}$
d. $\begin{array}{r} 55 \\ -29 \\ \hline \end{array}$
e. $\begin{array}{r} 49 \\ -18 \\ \hline \end{array}$

Part 7

a. $\begin{array}{r} \$3.82 \\ +1.29 \\ \hline \end{array}$
b. $\begin{array}{r} \$2.09 \\ +6.47 \\ \hline \end{array}$

Part 8　Independent Work

a. 9 x 4 = _____
b. 5 x 1 = _____
c. 9 x 2 = _____

d. 5 x 9 = _____
e. 5 x 4 = _____
f. 9 x 1 = _____

g. 10 x 3 = _____
h. 9 x 3 = _____
i. 5 x 4 = _____

j. 5 x 9 = _____
k. 9 x 4 = _____
l. 9 x 3 = _____

Part 9

a. □ ——28—→ 59
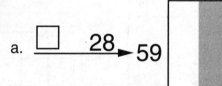

b. □ ——30—→ 47
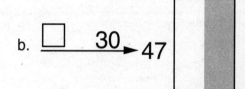

c. 48 ——49—→ □

d. 20 ——66—→ □

19

Test 1

Part 1

a. 3 + 9 = _____

b. 5 + 9 = _____

c. 8 + 9 = _____

d. 9 + 4 = _____

e. 9 + 6 = _____

f. 9 + 2 = _____

g. 9 + 7 = _____

Part 2

a. 4 + 6 = _____

b. 6 + 6 = _____

c. 3 + 6 = _____

d. 1 + 6 = _____

e. 5 + 6 = _____

f. 2 + 6 = _____

Part 3

a. 17 − 9 = _____

b. 14 − 9 = _____

c. 12 − 9 = _____

d. 15 − 9 = _____

e. 18 − 9 = _____

f. 13 − 9 = _____

Part 4

a. 3 + 3 = _____

b. 7 + 7 = _____

c. 6 + 6 = _____

d. 10 + 10 = _____

e. 2 + 2 = _____

f. 9 + 9 = _____

g. 5 + 5 = _____

h. 8 + 8 = _____

i. 4 + 4 = _____

j. 1 + 1 = _____

Part 5

a. 5 × 2 = _____

b. 2 × 3 = _____

c. 9 × 4 = _____

d. 5 × 1 = _____

e. 9 × 2 = _____

f. 5 × 9 = _____

g. 5 × 4 = _____

h. 9 × 1 = _____

i. 10 × 2 = _____

j. 9 × 3 = _____

Part 6 Write numbers on the arrows. Then write the multiplication problem and the answer. Remember to start with the column number.

a.
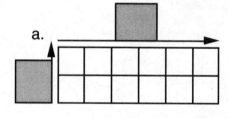

_____ squares

b.
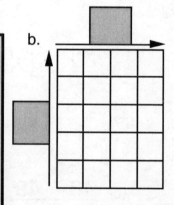

_____ squares

Part 7 Write the column problem and the answer for each family.

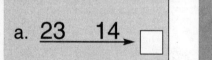

a. 23   14 → ☐

b. ☐   11 → 48

Part 8

a. 2 0 8
   + 6 0 9

b.   9 3
    + 2 9

20

Test 1/Extra Practice

a. 3
  +9

b. 5
  +9

c. 8
  +9

d. 9
  +4

e. 9
  +6

f. 9
  +2

g. 9
  +7

Part 2

a. 3 6 → ___

b. 4 6 → ___

c. 5 6 → ___

d. 6 6 → ___

e. 5 6 → ___

f. 3 6 → ___

g. 6 6 → ___

h. 4 6 → ___

i. 4 6 → ___

j. 6 6 → ___

k. 3 6 → ___

l. 5 6 → ___

_____

_____

_____

_____

Part 3

a. 15
  − 9

e. 18
  − 9

b. 17
  − 9

f. 11
  − 9

c. 13
  − 9

g. 14
  − 9

d. 16
  − 9

h. 12
  − 9

Part 4

a. 1 + 1 = ___

b. 2 + 2 = ___

c. 3 + 3 = ___

d. 4 + 4 = ___

e. 5 + 5 = ___

f. 6 + 6 = ___

g. 7 + 7 = ___

h. 8 + 8 = ___

i. 9 + 9 = ___

j. 10 + 10 = ___

k. 6 + 6 = ___

l. 9 + 9 = ___

m. 5 + 5 = ___

n. 3 + 3 = ___

o. 8 + 8 = ___

p. 10 + 10 = ___

q. 2 + 2 = ___

r. 4 + 4 = ___

s. 1 + 1 = ___

t. 7 + 7 = ___

a. $9 \times 6 =$ _____   b. $2 \times 6 =$ _____   c. $5 \times 6 =$ _____

d. $2 \times 4 =$ _____   e. $5 \times 4 =$ _____   f. $9 \times 4 =$ _____

Part 6

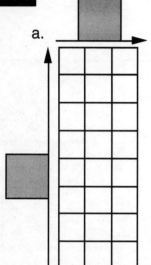
a.

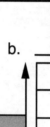
b.

_____ squares

_____ squares

Part 7

a.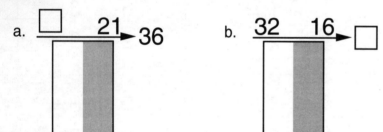

21 ➤ 36

b. 32   16 ➤ ☐

c. ☐   51 ➤ 71

d. 12   63 ➤ ☐

e.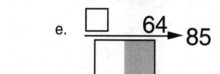

☐   64 ➤ 85

Part 8

a. 189   b. 42   c. 370   d. 609   e. 685   f. 356
  +133   +298   +298   +209   + 99   +292

22

Lesson 11

Part 1

a. $\underset{\longrightarrow}{2 \qquad 6}$ ___

b. $\underset{\longrightarrow}{5 \qquad 6}$ ___

c. $\underset{\longrightarrow}{6 \qquad 6}$ ___

d. $\underset{\longrightarrow}{4 \qquad 6}$ ___

e. $\underset{\longrightarrow}{1 \qquad 6}$ ___

f. $\underset{\longrightarrow}{5 \qquad 6}$ ___

g. $\underset{\longrightarrow}{3 \qquad 6}$ ___

h. $\underset{\longrightarrow}{2 \qquad 6}$ ___

Part 2

a. $1 \times 7 =$ ___

b. $1 \times 4 =$ ___

c. $1 \times 10 =$ ___

d. $1 \times 6 =$ ___

Part 3

a.
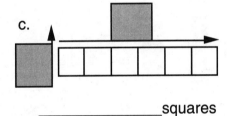

_____squares

b.
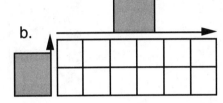

_____squares

c.
_____squares

d.
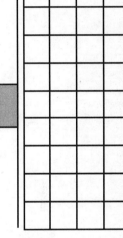

_____squares

Part 4

a. $\underset{\longrightarrow}{5 \qquad 6}$ ___

_____

_____

b. $\underset{\longrightarrow}{4 \qquad 6}$ ___

_____

_____

Part 5

a.
$$\begin{array}{r} 8\,4 \\ -\,2\,9 \\ \hline \end{array}$$

b.
$$\begin{array}{r} 8\,9 \\ -\,2\,8 \\ \hline \end{array}$$

c.
$$\begin{array}{r} 5\,3 \\ -\,4\,4 \\ \hline \end{array}$$

d.
$$\begin{array}{r} 2\,7 \\ -\,1\,6 \\ \hline \end{array}$$

e.
$$\begin{array}{r} 3\,1 \\ -\,1\,2 \\ \hline \end{array}$$

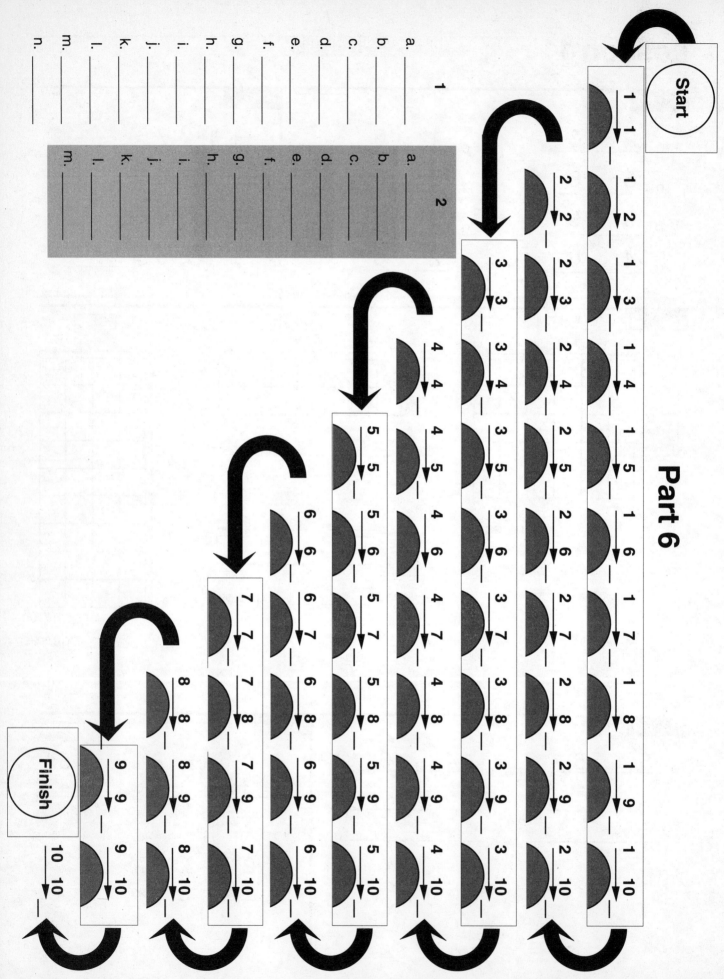

Part 6

Start

Finish

a. _____ 1
b. _____
c. _____
d. _____
e. _____
f. _____
g. _____
h. _____
i. _____
j. _____
k. _____
l. _____
m. _____
n. _____

a. _____ 2
b. _____
c. _____
d. _____
e. _____
f. _____
g. _____
h. _____
i. _____
j. _____
k. _____
l. _____
m. _____

Part 7

a. $4 + 6 =$ _____

b. $6 + 6 =$ _____

c. $3 + 6 =$ _____

d. $1 + 6 =$ _____

e. $5 + 6 =$ _____

f. $2 + 6 =$ _____

Part 8

a. $\begin{array}{r} 15 \\ -\ 6 \\ \hline \end{array}$

b. $\begin{array}{r} 15 \\ -\ 5 \\ \hline \end{array}$

c. $\begin{array}{r} 13 \\ -\ 3 \\ \hline \end{array}$

d. $\begin{array}{r} 17 \\ -\ 8 \\ \hline \end{array}$

e. $\begin{array}{r} 18 \\ -\ 9 \\ \hline \end{array}$

f. $\begin{array}{r} 14 \\ -\ 4 \\ \hline \end{array}$

g. $\begin{array}{r} 14 \\ -\ 5 \\ \hline \end{array}$

Part 9

a. $\begin{array}{r} \$1.25 \\ +\ 4.35 \\ \hline \end{array}$

b. $\begin{array}{r} \$8.86 \\ +\ 1.96 \\ \hline \end{array}$

c. $\begin{array}{r} \$2.04 \\ +\ 7.09 \\ \hline \end{array}$

Part 10

a. $\begin{array}{r} 7 \\ -\ 2 \\ \hline \end{array}$

b. $\begin{array}{r} 10 \\ -\ 2 \\ \hline \end{array}$

c. $\begin{array}{r} 4 \\ -\ 2 \\ \hline \end{array}$

d. $\begin{array}{r} 6 \\ -\ 2 \\ \hline \end{array}$

e. $\begin{array}{r} 9 \\ -\ 2 \\ \hline \end{array}$

f. $\begin{array}{r} 9 \\ -\ 1 \\ \hline \end{array}$

g. $\begin{array}{r} 9 \\ -\ 9 \\ \hline \end{array}$

h. $\begin{array}{r} 9 \\ -\ 8 \\ \hline \end{array}$

i. $\begin{array}{r} 9 \\ -\ 7 \\ \hline \end{array}$

j. $\begin{array}{r} 6 \\ -\ 5 \\ \hline \end{array}$

k. $\begin{array}{r} 6 \\ -\ 4 \\ \hline \end{array}$

l. $\begin{array}{r} 8 \\ -\ 8 \\ \hline \end{array}$

m. $\begin{array}{r} 8 \\ -\ 7 \\ \hline \end{array}$

n. $\begin{array}{r} 8 \\ -\ 6 \\ \hline \end{array}$

o. $\begin{array}{r} 10 \\ -\ 9 \\ \hline \end{array}$

p. $\begin{array}{r} 10 \\ -\ 8 \\ \hline \end{array}$

q. $\begin{array}{r} 10 \\ -\ 1 \\ \hline \end{array}$

r. $\begin{array}{r} 7 \\ -\ 7 \\ \hline \end{array}$

s. $\begin{array}{r} 7 \\ -\ 6 \\ \hline \end{array}$

t. $\begin{array}{r} 7 \\ -\ 5 \\ \hline \end{array}$

u. $\begin{array}{r} 8 \\ -\ 7 \\ \hline \end{array}$

Part 11

a. 53   23 → ☐

b. ☐   14 → 79

c. ☐   52 → 87

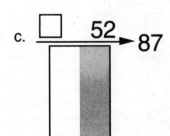

Lesson 12

Part 1

a.
$$
\begin{array}{r} 5\ 1 \\ -3\ 9 \\ \hline \end{array}
$$

b.
$$
\begin{array}{r} 6\ 7 \\ -1\ 7 \\ \hline \end{array}
$$

c.
$$
\begin{array}{r} 4\ 3 \\ -3\ 4 \\ \hline \end{array}
$$

d.
$$
\begin{array}{r} 7\ 5 \\ -6\ 4 \\ \hline \end{array}
$$

e.
$$
\begin{array}{r} 5\ 6 \\ -2\ 7 \\ \hline \end{array}
$$

Part 2

a. $6 + 5 =$ _____

b. $5 + 6 =$ _____

c. $6 + 1 =$ _____

d. $6 + 2 =$ _____

e. $1 + 6 =$ _____

f. $2 + 6 =$ _____

g. $6 + 6 =$ _____

h. $6 + 3 =$ _____

i. $6 + 4 =$ _____

j. $3 + 6 =$ _____

k. $4 + 6 =$ _____

Part 3   Independent Work

a.
$$
\begin{array}{r} \$\ 9.53 \\ -2.52 \\ \hline \end{array}
$$

b.
$$
\begin{array}{r} \$\ 8.75 \\ -6.50 \\ \hline \end{array}
$$

Part 4

a. $9 \times 4 =$ _____

b. $9 \times 3 =$ _____

c. $5 \times 3 =$ _____

d. $2 \times 3 =$ _____

e. $10 \times 3 =$ _____

f. $10 \times 5 =$ _____

g. $5 \times 10 =$ _____

h. $10 \times 2 =$ _____

i. $2 \times 10 =$ _____

j. $10 \times 10 =$ _____

k. $10 \times 9 =$ _____

l. $2 \times 9 =$ _____

Part 5

a.
$$
\begin{array}{r} 2\ 1\ 0 \\ 2\ 5\ 7 \\ +3\ 2\ 7 \\ \hline \end{array}
$$

b.
$$
\begin{array}{r} 1\ 1\ 1 \\ 3\ 2\ 7 \\ +4\ 4\ 9 \\ \hline \end{array}
$$

c.
$$
\begin{array}{r} 1\ 0\ 9 \\ 1\ 5\ 6 \\ +6\ 6\ 0 \\ \hline \end{array}
$$

d.
$$
\begin{array}{r} 1\ 1\ 5 \\ 4\ 6\ 5 \\ +2\ 8\ 5 \\ \hline \end{array}
$$

Part 6

a.
$$
\begin{array}{r} 1\ 5 \\ -\ 6 \\ \hline \end{array}
$$

b.
$$
\begin{array}{r} 1\ 6 \\ -\ 6 \\ \hline \end{array}
$$

c.
$$
\begin{array}{r} 1\ 5 \\ -\ 5 \\ \hline \end{array}
$$

d.
$$
\begin{array}{r} 1\ 7 \\ -\ 7 \\ \hline \end{array}
$$

e.
$$
\begin{array}{r} 1\ 7 \\ -\ 8 \\ \hline \end{array}
$$

f.
$$
\begin{array}{r} 1\ 3 \\ -\ 3 \\ \hline \end{array}
$$

g.
$$
\begin{array}{r} 1\ 8 \\ -\ 9 \\ \hline \end{array}
$$

h.
$$
\begin{array}{r} 1\ 8 \\ -\ 8 \\ \hline \end{array}
$$

Lesson 13

Part 1

a. □ → 9 → 17

b. 18 □ → 28

c. □ → 6 → 8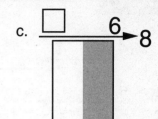

d. □ → 25 → 56

e. 14 □ → 76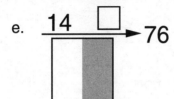

Part 2

a. 8 6
  − 5 7

b. 8 5
  − 6 4

c. 9 5
  − 2 0

d. 5 2
  − 4 9

e. 8 9
  − 2 7

f. 7 4
  − 4 5

Part 3

a. 1 x 3 = _____

b. 1 x 4 = _____

c. 1 x 7 = _____

d. 1 x 31 = _____

e. 1 x 1 = _____

Part 4   Independent Work

a. 3 + 6 = _____

b. 4 + 6 = _____

c. 6 + 6 = _____

d. 5 + 6 = _____

e. 6 + 2 = _____

f. 6 + 4 = _____

g. 6 + 5 = _____

h. 6 + 3 = _____

Part 5

a. 2 7 8
  + 3 4 9

b. 2 4 6
  + 4 5 4

c. 3 4 6
  + 2 6 5

d. 4 3 8
  + 3 6 8

Part 6

a. 9 x 2 = _____

b. 2 x 9 = _____

c. 2 x 5 = _____

d. 5 x 2 = _____

Part 7

a. 4 → 6 → __

b. 3 → 9 → __

Lesson 14

a. 4   4 ⟶ ___   f. 4   5 ⟶ ___   k. 4   6 ⟶ ___ _____

b. 4   5 ⟶ ___   g. 4   7 ⟶ ___   l. 4   5 ⟶ ___ _____

c. 4   6 ⟶ ___   h. 4   4 ⟶ ___   m. 4   4 ⟶ ___ _____

d. 4   7 ⟶ ___   i. 4   6 ⟶ ___   n. 4   7 ⟶ ___ _____

e. 4   8 ⟶ ___   j. 4   8 ⟶ ___   o. 4   8 ⟶ ___ _____

Part 2

a. 1 x 46 = _____   b. 1 x 3 = _____   c. 17 x 1 = _____

d. 1 x 20 = _____   e. 1 x 1 = _____   f. 15 x 1 = _____

Part 3

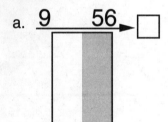

a. 9   56 ⟶ ☐

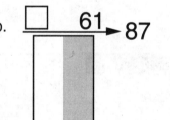

b. ☐   61 ⟶ 87

c. 23   ☐ ⟶ 74

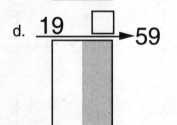

d. 19   ☐ ⟶ 59

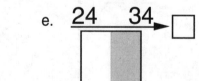

e. 24   34 ⟶ ☐

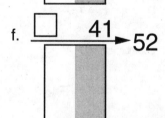

f. ☐   41 ⟶ 52

Part 4   Independent Work

a.	b.	c.	d.	e.	f.	g.
5 7	7 5	6 7	8 7	9 5	5 4	5 3
− 4 7	− 6 9	− 4 8	− 2 9	− 6 6	− 4 3	− 4 4

Lesson 15

Part 1

a.
```
  346
- 139
```

b.
```
  675
- 449
```

c.
```
  315
- 114
```

d.
```
  324
- 215
```

e.
```
  359
- 348
```

Part 2

a. 4 → 4 ___

b. 4 → 5 ___

c. 4 → 6 ___

d. 4 → 7 ___

e. 4 → 8 ___

f. 4 → 5 ___

g. 4 → 8 ___

h. 4 → 7 ___

i. 4 → 4 ___

j. 4 → 6 ___

k. 4 → 7 ___

l. 4 → 5 ___

m. 4 → 8 ___

n. 4 → 6 ___

o. 4 → 4 ___

Part 3

6	6	1	
2	3	2	
1	1	2	

Part 4

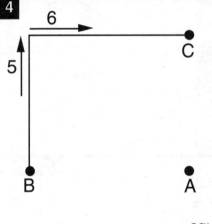

_____ squares

Part 5 Independent Work

a. 5 x 3 = _____

b. 10 x 3 = _____

c. 9 x 3 = _____

d. 2 x 3 = _____

Part 6

a.
```
  235
+ 666
```

b.
```
  177
+ 687
```

c.
```
  235
+ 445
```

d.
```
  177
+ 268
```

Lesson 16

Part 1

a. 4   6 → _____

b. 4   8 → _____

c. 4   5 → _____

d. 4   7 → _____

e. 4   4 → _____

f. 4   5 → _____

g. 4   8 → _____

h. 4   6 → _____

i. 4   4 → _____

j. 4   7 → _____

Part 2

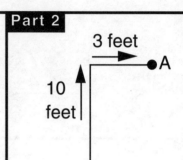

_____

Part 3

a.
$$\begin{array}{r} 656 \\ -527 \\ \hline \end{array}$$

b.
$$\begin{array}{r} 924 \\ -719 \\ \hline \end{array}$$

c.
$$\begin{array}{r} 675 \\ -329 \\ \hline \end{array}$$

d.
$$\begin{array}{r} 724 \\ -503 \\ \hline \end{array}$$

Part 4

2	1	9	
2	3	1	
5	5	6	

Part 5
Independent Work

a. $2 \times 2 =$ _____

b. $2 \times 3 =$ _____

c. $5 \times 2 =$ _____

d. $5 \times 3 =$ _____

e. $10 \times 2 =$ _____

f. $9 \times 2 =$ _____

Part 6

a. $4 + 5 =$ _____

b. $4 + 8 =$ _____

c. $4 + 4 =$ _____

d. $5 + 6 =$ _____

e. $4 + 10 =$ _____

f. $4 + 8 =$ _____

g. $9 + 1 =$ _____

h. $2 + 6 =$ _____

i. $4 + 7 =$ _____

j. $6 + 6 =$ _____

k. $4 + 7 =$ _____

l. $4 + 5 =$ _____

m. $4 + 4 =$ _____

n. $4 + 10 =$ _____

o. $4 + 6 =$ _____

Lesson 17

a. $\dfrac{4 \qquad 8}{\qquad} \rightarrow 12$

_____

_____

b. $\dfrac{4 \qquad 7}{\qquad} \rightarrow 11$

_____

_____

Part 2

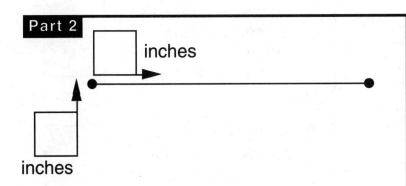

inches

inches

_____

Part 3

4	6	9	
2	9	1	
1	1	4	

Part 4   **Independent Work**

a. $4 + 8 =$ _____   b. $8 + 4 =$ _____   c. $4 + 5 =$ _____

d. $4 + 7 =$ _____   e. $6 + 4 =$ _____   f. $4 + 9 =$ _____

g. $6 + 4 =$ _____   h. $5 + 4 =$ _____   i. $4 + 7 =$ _____

j. $8 + 4 =$ _____   k. $4 + 4 =$ _____   l. $9 + 4 =$ _____

Part 5

a. $\begin{array}{r} 284 \\ +696 \\ \hline \end{array}$

b. $\begin{array}{r} 566 \\ +174 \\ \hline \end{array}$

c. $\begin{array}{r} 346 \\ +465 \\ \hline \end{array}$

Lesson 18

a. 6 8 <u>3</u>   b. 6 <u>8</u> 3   c. 4 7 <u>1</u>   d. 4 <u>7</u> 1

Part 2

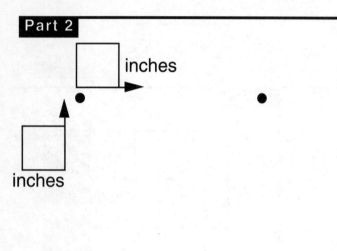

Part 3

a. The store had 31 bottles. Then it sold 20 bottles. How many bottles did it end up with?

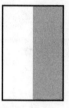

b. A boy had 53 marbles. The boy bought 21 more marbles. How many marbles did the boy end up with?

c. A girl had 53 papers. Then she delivered 32 papers. How many papers did the girl end up with?

d. A girl had 51 books. Then she sold 19 books. How many books did she end up with?

e. A boy had 51 books. Then he bought 19 more books. How many books did he end up with?

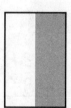

Part 4

This table shows the number of cars that went down different streets.

	Elm Street	Oak Street	Maple Street	Total for all streets
Red cars	4	5	9	
Yellow cars	2	2	8	
Blue cars	4	4	1	
Total for all cars				

a. $ 7.67
  − 2.39

b. $ 5.76
  − .67

c. $ 5.53
  − 3.29

d. $ 4.24
  − 2.19

Part 6

a. 2 x 4 = ____

b. 10 x 4 = ____

c. 5 x 4 = ____

d. 9 x 4 = ____

Part 7

a. $ 6.86
  + 2.59

b. $ 7.54
  + 1.45

c. $ 2.67
  + 2.39

d. $ 2.59
  + 6.94

Lesson 19

Part 1

a. 4 6 <u>8</u>

b. 4 <u>6</u> 8

c. 9 3 <u>1</u>

d. 9 <u>3</u> 1

Part 2

a. The big number is a box. The small numbers are 13 and 52.

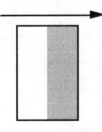

b. The first small number is 18. The second small number is a box. The big number is 79.

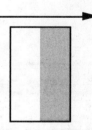

c. The first small number is a box. The second small number is 21. The big number is 86.

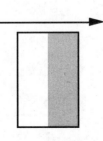

d. The first small number is 41. The big number is a box. The second small number is 28.

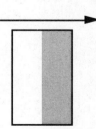

a. 5 5 ___
b. 5 6 ___
c. 5 7 ___
d. 5 8 ___
e. 5 9 ___

f. 5 8 ___
g. 5 6 ___
h. 5 9 ___
i. 5 5 ___
j. 5 7 ___

k. 5 9 ___
l. 5 6 ___
m. 5 8 ___
n. 5 7 ___
o. 5 5 ___

This table shows how much rain fell in different cities.

	May	June	July	Total for all months
River City	6	9	1	
Hill Town	3	1	8	
Oak Grove	0	7	9	
Total for all cities				

Lesson 20

a. 5 5 ___
b. 5 6 ___
c. 5 7 ___
d. 5 8 ___
e. 5 9 ___

f. 5 7 ___
g. 5 9 ___
h. 5 6 ___
i. 5 8 ___
j. 5 5 ___

34

Part 2

a. The first small number is 50. The big number is 77. The second small number is a box.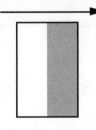

b. The first small number is 26. The second small number is 59. The big number is a box.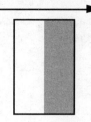

c. The second small number is a box. The big number is 81. The first small number is 61.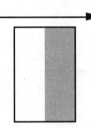

d. The big number is 96. The first small number is a box. The second small number is 75.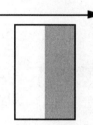

Part 3

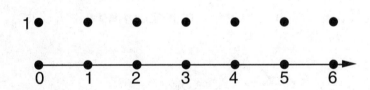

Part 4

a.
```
  475
- 193
-----
    2
```

b.
```
  869
- 572
-----
    7
```

c.
```
  957
- 661
-----
```

d.
```
  583
- 391
-----
```

Part 5 — Independent Work

a. 10 x 10 = _____

b. 2 x 10 = _____

c. 5 x 10 = _____

d. 9 x 10 = _____

e. 5 x 1 = _____

f. 2 x 1 = _____

g. 1 x 7 = _____

h. 1 x 46 = _____

Part 6

a.
```
  756
+  65
```

b.
```
  283
+ 367
```

c.
```
  464
+ 465
```

d.
```
  545
+ 355
```

Test 2

a. 4 + 5 = _____   b. 4 + 8 = _____   c. 4 + 4 = _____

d. 5 + 6 = _____   e. 4 + 10 = _____   f. 9 + 1 = _____

g. 2 + 6 = _____   h. 4 + 7 = _____   i. 6 + 6 = _____

j. 4 + 5 = _____   k. 4 + 6 = _____

Part 2 Work the area problems. Write the multiplication problem and the whole answer.

a.
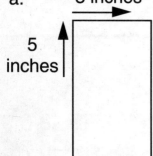
3 inches

5 inches

_____

b.
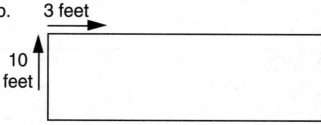
3 feet

10 feet

_____

Part 3

This table shows how much rain fell in different cities during May, June and July. Fill in the totals.

	May	June	July	Total for all months
River City	6	9	1	
Hill Town	3	1	8	
Oak Grove	0	7	9	
Total for all cities				

Write each problem in a column. Copy the amounts that are shown.
Add and write the answer.

a. $2.36 $1.11 $2.20

b. $3.29 $1.79 $2.01

Complete the number family for each problem. Then write the addition problem or the subtraction problem and the answer.

a. The big number is a box. The first small number is 38. The second small number is 39.

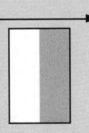

b. The first small number is 50. The big number is 77. The second small number is a box.

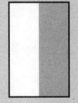

c. The second small number is 29. The first small number is a box. The big number is 96.

a. 355
  − 149
  _____

b. 894
  − 685
  _____

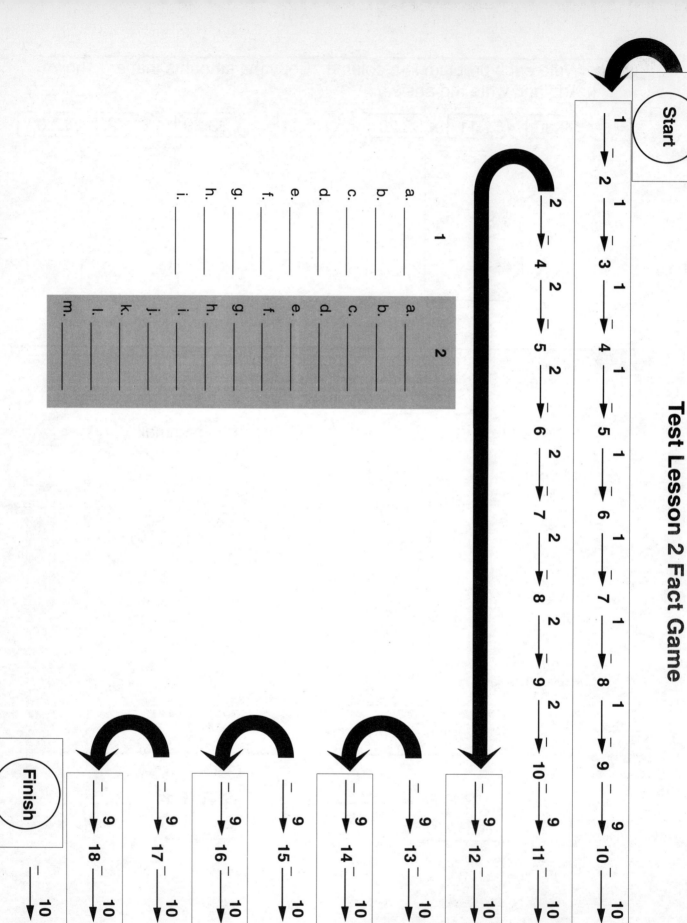

Test 2/Extra Practice

a. 4   6 → ___

b. 4   8 → ___

c. 4   5 → ___

d. 4   7 → ___

e. 4   4 → ___

f. 4   5 → ___

g. 4   8 → ___

h. 4   6 → ___

i. 4   4 → ___

j. 4   7 → ___

Part 2

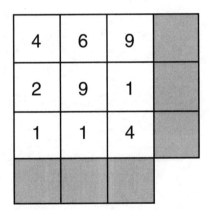

4	6	9	
2	9	1	
1	1	4	

Part 3

a. The big number is a box. The small numbers are 13 and 52.

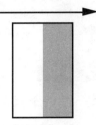

b. The first small number is 18. The second small number is a box. The big number is 79.

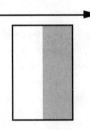

c. The first small number is a box. The second small number is 21. The big number is 86.

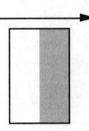

d. The first small number is 41. The big number is a box. The second small number is 28.

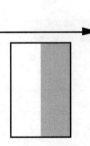

Part 4

a.
```
  346
- 139
```

b.
```
  675
- 449
```

c.
```
  315
- 114
```

d.
```
  324
- 215
```

e.
```
  359
- 348
```

Lesson 21

Part 1

a. 3<u>7</u>8   b. 37<u>8</u>   c. 4<u>6</u>2   d. 46<u>2</u>

Part 2

a.
```
  4 6 6
- 1 9 5
      1
```

b.
```
  5 7 0
- 4 8 0
      0
```

c.
```
  2 4 3
-   9 1
```

Part 3

a. 5 → 8 ___   f. 5 → 6 ___

b. 5 → 5 ___   g. 5 → 5 ___

c. 5 → 7 ___   h. 5 → 8 ___

d. 5 → 6 ___   i. 5 → 7 ___

e. 5 → 9 ___   j. 5 → 9 ___

Part 4

Part 5

a. 7—6   b. 5—9

c. 56—59   d. 305—35

e. 20—200

Part 6   Independent Work

a.
```
  4 8 6
+ 3 7 9
```

b.
```
  2 4 9
+ 3 9 8
```

c.
```
  1 4 5
+ 6 5 6
```

d.
```
  2 3 2
+ 5 5 8
```

40

a. $1 \times 46 =$ _____   b. $5 \times 1 =$ _____   c. $1 \times 5 =$ _____

d. $6 \times 1 =$ _____   e. $1 \times 6 =$ _____   f. $18 \times 1 =$ _____

Part 8

a. The small numbers are 63 and a box. The big number is 92.

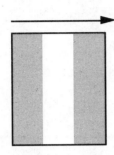

b. The second small number is 409. The big number is a box. The first small number is 196.

c. The big number is 284. The first small number is a box. The second small number is 254.

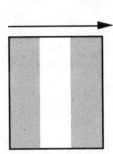

d. The small numbers are 182 and 509. The big number is a box.

Lesson 22

Part 1

9

3

Part 2

a. $406 - 46$ b. $406 - 460$

c. $86 - 91$ d. $40 - 400$

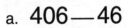

a. 465
−174

b. 707
−424

c. 676
−282

d. 778
−295

Part 4   Independent Work

a. 9 x 3 = _____   b. 9 x 4 = _____   c. 9 x 5 = _____

d. 5 x 3 = _____   e. 5 x 4 = _____   f. 5 x 5 = _____

g. 10 x 3 = _____   h. 10 x 4 = _____   i. 10 x 5 = _____

Part 5

a. 3 3 5   b. 2 3 7   c. 2 5 4   d. 6 7 7
   + 5 5 5   + 3 8 7   + 5 6 8   + 2 3 4

Do the independent work for Lesson 22 of your textbook.

Lesson 23

Part 1

① ② ③

a. ⎯ 4 → 5   e. ⎯ 4 → 7   i. ⎯ 4 → 8   _____

b. ⎯ 4 → 6   f. ⎯ 4 → 6   j. ⎯ 4 → 6   _____

c. ⎯ 4 → 7   g. ⎯ 4 → 8   k. ⎯ 4 → 7   _____

d. ⎯ 4 → 8   h. ⎯ 4 → 5   l. ⎯ 4 → 5   _____

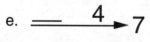
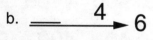

Part 2

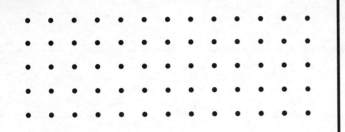

5

7

Part 3

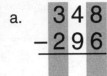

a.
```
  3 4 8
- 2 9 6
```

b.
```
  6 5 7
- 4 1 9
```

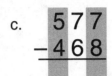

c.
```
  5 7 7
- 4 6 8
```

d.
```
  7 3 2
- 2 9 2
```

Part 5

a. 5 + 7 = 12

b. 5 + 9 = 14

c. 5 + 5 = 10

d. 5 + 8 = 13

e. 5 + 6 = 11

f. 4 + 5 = 9

g. 2 + 5 = 7

h. 8 + 5 = 13

i. 6 + 5 = 11

j. 10 + 5 = 15

k. 7 + 5 = 12

l. 3 + 5 = 8

m. 9 + 5 = 14

n. 8 + 5 = 13

o. 7 + 5 = 12

Part 4

a. ●————— 3 inches —————●

●—— 4 inches

2 inches

b.

3 inches

c. ●—— 2 inches ——●

2 inches

Lesson 24

Part 1

a. 6   6 → ___

b. 6   7 → ___

c. 6   8 → ___

d. 6   9 → ___

e. 6   8 → ___

f. 6   6 → ___

g. 6   9 → ___

h. 6   7 → ___

i. 6   9 → ___

j. 6   7 → ___

k. 6   6 → ___

l. 6   8 → ___

Part 2

a. • 1 inch •

• 4 inches

b. •
3 inches | 2 inches •

c. • 2 inches •   ↓ 2 inches

Part 3

①

a. ═══ 4 → 6

b. ═══ 4 → 5

c. ═══ 4 → 8

d. ═══ 4 → 7

②

e. ═══ 4 → 8

f. ═══ 4 → 6

g. ═══ 4 → 5

h. ═══ 4 → 7

③

i. ═══ 4 → 8

j. ═══ 4 → 6

k. ═══ 4 → 5

l. ═══ 4 → 7

44

Part 4

a. $\begin{array}{r} 537 \\ -297 \\ \hline \end{array}$
b. $\begin{array}{r} 553 \\ -260 \\ \hline \end{array}$
c. $\begin{array}{r} 756 \\ -547 \\ \hline \end{array}$
d. $\begin{array}{r} 246 \\ -152 \\ \hline \end{array}$
e. $\begin{array}{r} 608 \\ -596 \\ \hline \end{array}$
f. $\begin{array}{r} 389 \\ -98 \\ \hline \end{array}$

Part 5 — Independent Work

a. $2 \times 4 = \underline{\quad}$ b. $5 \times 4 = \underline{\quad}$ c. $10 \times 7 = \underline{\quad}$

d. $9 \times 4 = \underline{\quad}$ e. $5 \times 7 = \underline{\quad}$ f. $2 \times 7 = \underline{\quad}$

g. $10 \times 4 = \underline{\quad}$ h. $9 \times 7 = \underline{\quad}$ i. $9 \times 4 = \underline{\quad}$

Do the independent work for Lesson 24 of your textbook.

Lesson 25

Part 1

a. J is less than M.

b. R is more than P.

c. P is more than J.

d. W is less than J.

Part 2

a. 6 _____ 9 _____

b. 6 _____ 8 _____

c. 6 _____ 7 _____

d. 6 _____ 6 _____

e. 6 _____ 7 _____

f. 6 _____ 9 _____

g. 6 _____ 6 _____

h. 6 _____ 8 _____

Part 3

a. $5 - 4 = \underline{\quad}$ e. $5 - 4 = \underline{\quad}$

b. $6 - 4 = \underline{\quad}$ f. $7 - 4 = \underline{\quad}$

c. $8 - 4 = \underline{\quad}$ g. $8 - 4 = \underline{\quad}$

d. $7 - 4 = \underline{\quad}$ h. $6 - 4 = \underline{\quad}$

a. $6 + 4 =$ _____   b. $9 + 4 =$ _____   c. $7 + 4 =$ _____

d. $5 + 4 =$ _____   e. $8 + 4 =$ _____   f. $6 + 6 =$ _____

g. $6 + 9 =$ _____   h. $6 + 7 =$ _____   i. $6 + 5 =$ _____

j. $6 + 8 =$ _____   k. $4 + 4 =$ _____   l. $7 + 7 =$ _____

m. $8 + 8 =$ _____   n. $5 + 5 =$ _____   o. $3 + 3 =$ _____

Do the independent work for Lesson 25 of your textbook.

Lesson 26

Part 1

a. $7 - 5 =$ _____   b. $7 - 4 =$ _____   c. $9 - 2 =$ _____

d. $8 - 4 =$ _____   e. $10 - 9 =$ _____   f. $7 - 6 =$ _____

g. $8 - 4 =$ _____   h. $6 - 2 =$ _____   i. $7 - 3 =$ _____

j. $9 - 1 =$ _____   k. $7 - 5 =$ _____   l. $7 - 4 =$ _____

m. $3 - 1 =$ _____   n. $7 - 5 =$ _____   o. $8 - 4 =$ _____

Part 2

a. $6 \quad 9 \longrightarrow$ ___   f. $5 \quad 6 \longrightarrow$ ___

b. $4 \quad 6 \longrightarrow$ ___   g. $6 \quad 8 \longrightarrow$ ___

c. $6 \quad 6 \longrightarrow$ ___   h. $6 \quad 9 \longrightarrow$ ___

d. $6 \quad 8 \longrightarrow$ ___   i. $6 \quad 7 \longrightarrow$ ___

e. $6 \quad 7 \longrightarrow$ ___   j. $6 \quad 6 \longrightarrow$ ___

Part 3   Independent Work

a. $5 \times 9 =$ _____

b. $2 \times 9 =$ _____

c. $1 \times 9 =$ _____

d. $10 \times 9 =$ _____

e. $9 \times 9 =$ _____

f. $9 \times 5 =$ _____

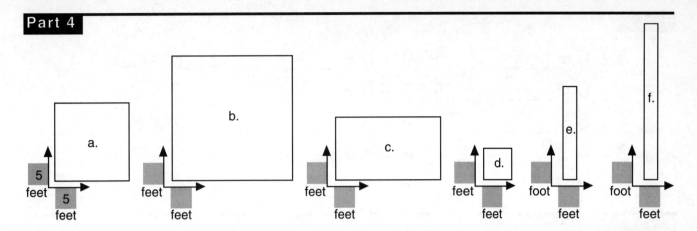

Description 1: The rectangle is 10 feet high and 1 foot wide.

_____

Description 2: The rectangle is 4 feet high and 7 feet wide.

_____

Description 3: The rectangle is 2 feet high and 2 feet wide.

_____

Description 4: The rectangle is 8 feet high and 8 feet wide.

_____

Lesson 27

Part 1

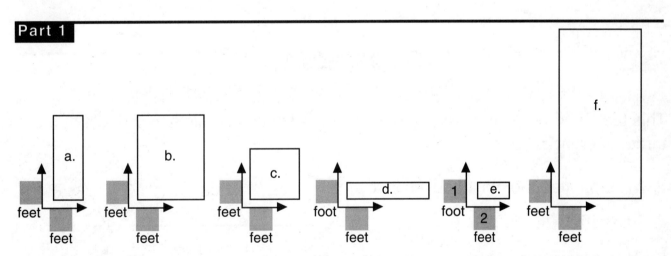

Description 1: The rectangle is 5 feet wide and 1 foot high.

_____

Description 2: The rectangle is 2 feet wide and 5 feet high.

_____

Description 3: The rectangle is 5 feet wide and 10 feet high.

_____

Description 4: The rectangle is 3 feet wide and 3 feet high.

_____

Part 2

a. $9 + 6 = \underline{\hspace{1cm}}$ b. $8 + 6 = \underline{\hspace{1cm}}$ c. $5 + 6 = \underline{\hspace{1cm}}$

d. $6 + 6 = \underline{\hspace{1cm}}$ e. $7 + 6 = \underline{\hspace{1cm}}$ f. $10 + 6 = \underline{\hspace{1cm}}$

g. $4 + 6 = \underline{\hspace{1cm}}$ h. $2 + 6 = \underline{\hspace{1cm}}$ i. $7 + 6 = \underline{\hspace{1cm}}$

j. $3 + 6 = \underline{\hspace{1cm}}$ k. $8 + 6 = \underline{\hspace{1cm}}$ l. $6 + 7 = \underline{\hspace{1cm}}$

m. $6 + 8 = \underline{\hspace{1cm}}$ n. $6 + 9 = \underline{\hspace{1cm}}$ o. $10 + 6 = \underline{\hspace{1cm}}$

Part 3

a. •——————————• 3 inches

•—

2 inches

b. •——————• 1 inch   ↓ 1 inch

Part 4

a. $8 - 4 = 4$ b. $6 - 4 = 2$ c. $5 - 4 = 1$ d. $4 - 3 = 1$

e. $7 - 4 = 3$ f. $8 - 4 = 4$ g. $8 - 6 = 2$ h. $8 - 7 = 1$

i. $4 - 4 = 0$ j. $6 - 4 = 2$ k. $8 - 4 = 4$ l. $7 - 4 = 3$

m. $7 - 5 = 2$ n. $7 - 6 = 1$ o. $8 - 4 = 4$

Part 5   Independent Work

Fill in the totals. Then write the answers to the questions.

This table shows the number of houses painted in June, July and August by three different people.

a. Who painted the most houses in the three months? _____.

b. The largest number of houses were painted in the month of _____.

c. The fewest number of houses were painted in the month of _____.

	June	July	August	Total for all months
Sid	7	7	2	
Rosa	2	5	10	
James	9	2	1	
Total for all people				

Part 6

a. 301 — 310   b. 560 — 559   c. 370 — 307   d. 699 — 700

Do the independent work for Lesson 27 of your textbook.

Lesson 28

Part 1

a. J is ⑤ less than K. ——————→

b. J is ⑱ more than K. ——————→

c. P is ⑨ less than T. ——————→

d. H is ⑫ larger than F. ——————→

e. H is ⑰ less than Y. ——————→

Part 2

a. D ∠ 12

| 14 | 12 | 10 | 4 |

b. D ⋝ 14

| 12 | 15 | 10 | 17 |

c. ☐ ∠ 20

| 13 | 17 | 21 | 19 |

d. ☐ ⋝ 20

| 13 | 17 | 21 | 19 |

Part 3

a. The rectangle is 4 feet wide and 2 feet high.

b. The rectangle is 3 feet high and 5 feet wide.

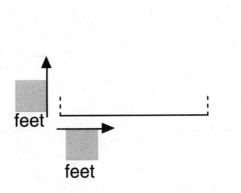

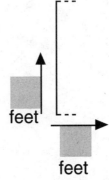

Draw the rectangle. Write the multiplication problem and the answer. Remember the units in the answer.

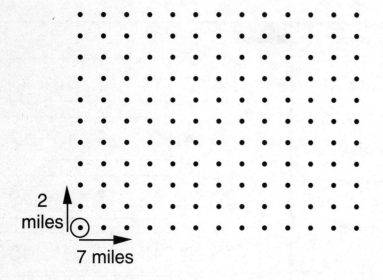

2 miles

7 miles

a. $\begin{array}{r} 317 \\ -186 \\ \hline \end{array}$

b. $\begin{array}{r} 586 \\ -417 \\ \hline \end{array}$

c. $\begin{array}{r} 509 \\ -324 \\ \hline \end{array}$

d. $\begin{array}{r} 475 \\ -409 \\ \hline \end{array}$

Part 6   Write the time for each clock.

a.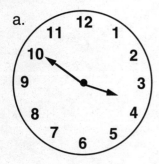

b.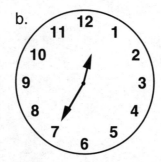

c.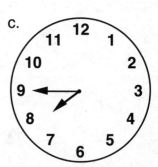

Do the independent work for Lesson 28 of your textbook.

Lesson 29

Part 1

a. $\equiv \xrightarrow{5} 7$ e. $\equiv \xrightarrow{5} 10$ i. $\equiv \xrightarrow{5} 8$

b. $\equiv \xrightarrow{5} 8$ f. $\equiv \xrightarrow{5} 7$ j. $\equiv \xrightarrow{5} 10$

c. $\equiv \xrightarrow{5} 9$ g. $\equiv \xrightarrow{5} 8$ k. $\equiv \xrightarrow{5} 7$

d. $\equiv \xrightarrow{5} 10$ h. $\equiv \xrightarrow{5} 9$ l. $\equiv \xrightarrow{5} 9$

Part 2

a. $\begin{array}{r} 205 \\ -115 \\ \hline \end{array}$ b. $\begin{array}{r} 610 \\ -290 \\ \hline \end{array}$ c. $\begin{array}{r} 983 \\ -474 \\ \hline \end{array}$ d. $\begin{array}{r} 803 \\ -751 \\ \hline \end{array}$

Part 3

a. The rectangle is 5 feet high and 7 feet wide.

b. The rectangle is 5 feet high and 4 feet wide.

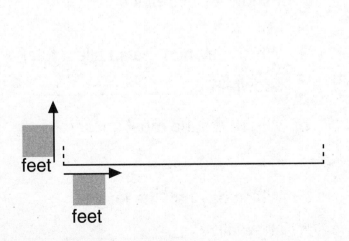

feet

feet

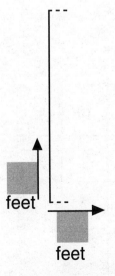

feet

feet

a. $\begin{array}{r} 130 \\ 36 \\ +568 \\ \hline \end{array}$ b. $\begin{array}{r} 17 \\ 421 \\ +375 \\ \hline \end{array}$ c. $\begin{array}{r} 146 \\ 200 \\ +385 \\ \hline \end{array}$ d. $\begin{array}{r} 246 \\ 21 \\ +567 \\ \hline \end{array}$

Part 5 Write the column problem and the answer.

a. A man had 344 pounds of sand. He bought 287 more pounds of sand. How many pounds of sand did he end up with?

b. A woman had 556 pounds of sand. She got 368 more pounds of sand. How many pounds of sand did she end up with?

c. A man had 760 pounds of sand. He used up 232 pounds of sand. How many pounds of sand did he have left?

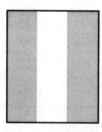

Part 6

a. $2 \times 9 =$ _____   b. $9 \times 2 =$ _____   c. $10 \times 5 =$ _____

d. $5 \times 7 =$ _____   e. $9 \times 3 =$ _____   f. $5 \times 8 =$ _____

Part 7 Fill in the totals. Then answer each question.

	Monday	Wednesday	Thursday	Total for all days
Snow Pass	0	1	10	
White Butte	0	3	9	
River Lodge	9	4	7	
Total for all towns				

This table shows how many inches of snow fell in 3 places.

a. Which day had the smallest total snowfall? _____

b. Where did the most snow fall?

_____

c. Which day had the largest snowfall? _____

Lesson 30

Part 1

a. R $\angle$ 15 | 17   15   13   1 |

b. T $\succeq$ 300 | 390   300   150   580 |

c. J $\angle$ 300 | 290   300   150   580 |

d. K $\succeq$ 56 | 50   59   57   60 |

Part 2

a. The rectangle is 9 miles high and 5 miles wide.

b. The rectangle is 10 miles high and 3 miles wide.

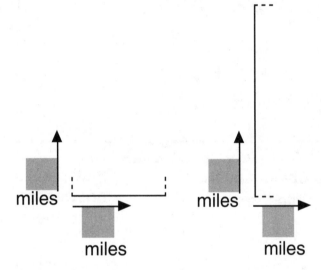

miles   miles   miles   miles

Part 3

a. $\xrightarrow{5}$ 10

b. $\xrightarrow{5}$ 9

c. $\xrightarrow{5}$ 8

d. $\xrightarrow{5}$ 7

e. $\xrightarrow{5}$ 9

f. $\xrightarrow{5}$ 10

g. $\xrightarrow{5}$ 7

h. $\xrightarrow{5}$ 8

i. $\xrightarrow{5}$ 7

j. $\xrightarrow{5}$ 10

k. $\xrightarrow{5}$ 8

l. $\xrightarrow{5}$ 9

Part 4

a.
```
  991
- 233
```

b.
```
  507
-  56
```

c.
```
  850
- 741
```

Do the independent work for Lesson 30 of your textbook.

Test 3

Part 1

a. $8 - 4 =$ _____   b. $6 - 4 =$ _____   c. $5 - 4 =$ _____

d. $4 - 3 =$ _____   e. $7 - 4 =$ _____   f. $8 - 4 =$ _____

g. $8 - 6 =$ _____   h. $8 - 7 =$ _____   i. $4 - 4 =$ _____

j. $7 - 5 =$ _____   k. $7 - 6 =$ _____

Part 2

a. $5 + 7 =$ _____   b. $5 + 9 =$ _____   c. $5 + 5 =$ _____

d. $5 + 8 =$ _____   e. $5 + 6 =$ _____   f. $4 + 5 =$ _____

g. $2 + 5 =$ _____   h. $8 + 5 =$ _____   i. $6 + 5 =$ _____

j. $10 + 5 =$ _____   k. $7 + 5 =$ _____   l. $3 + 5 =$ _____

m. $9 + 5 =$ _____   n. $5 + 4 =$ _____

Part 3 Draw the rectangle. Write the multiplication problem and the answer. Then write the correct unit.

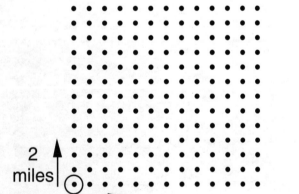

2 miles

7 miles

_____

Part 4 Draw the rectangle. Write the multiplication problem and the answer for the rectangle. Then write the correct unit.

a. The rectangle is 4 feet wide and 10 feet high.

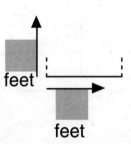

feet

feet

_____

Go to Test 3 in your textbook.

54

Test 3/Extra Practice

a. 5 − 4 = _____

b. 6 − 4 = _____

c. 8 − 4 = _____

d. 7 − 4 = _____

e. 5 − 4 = _____

f. 7 − 4 = _____

g. 8 − 4 = _____

h. 6 − 4 = _____

_____

Part 2

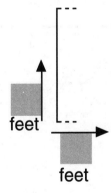

Part 3

a. The rectangle is 4 feet wide and 2 feet high.

b. The rectangle is 3 feet high and 5 feet wide.

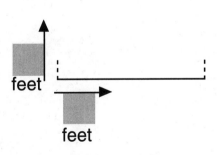

feet

feet

feet

feet

_____

55

a. J is ⑤ less than K. ⟶

b. J is ⑱ more than K. ⟶

c. P is ⑨ less than T. ⟶

d. H is ⑫ larger than F. ⟶

e. H is ⑰ less than Y. ⟶

Part 5

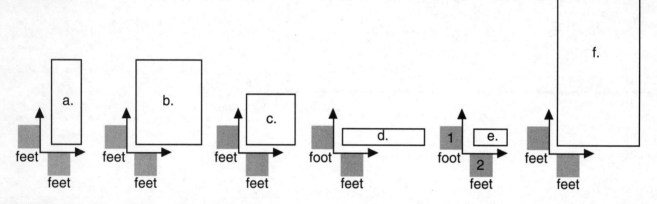

Description 1: The rectangle is 5 feet wide and 1 foot high.

_____

Description 2: The rectangle is 2 feet wide and 5 feet high.

_____

Description 3: The rectangle is 5 feet wide and 10 feet high.

_____

Description 4: The rectangle is 3 feet wide and 3 feet high.

_____

Part 6

a.
```
  348
- 296
```

b.
```
  657
- 419
```

c.
```
  577
- 468
```

d.
```
  732
- 292
```

Part 7

a.
```
  130
   36
+ 568
```

b.
```
   17
  421
+ 375
```

c.
```
  146
  200
+ 385
```

d.
```
  246
   21
+ 567
```

Lesson 31

Part 1

a. 657
  −449

b. 717
  −408

c. 432
  −392

d. 808
  −387

Part 2

a. The rectangle is 9 feet wide and 2 feet high.

b. The rectangle is 10 feet high and 1 foot wide.

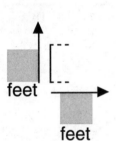

feet

feet

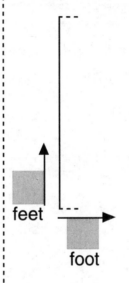

feet

foot

Part 3

a. ═══ 5 ➤ 9

b. ═══ 5 ➤ 10

c. ═══ 5 ➤ 8

d. ═══ 5 ➤ 7

e. ═══ 5 ➤ 10

f. ═══ 5 ➤ 9

g. ═══ 5 ➤ 8

h. ═══ 5 ➤ 7

i. ═══ 5 ➤ 10

j. ═══ 5 ➤ 8

k. ═══ 5 ➤ 7

l. ═══ 5 ➤ 9

Part 4   Independent Work

a. 357
  +378

b. 274
  +648

c. 556
  +265

d. 466
  +378

Do the independent work for Lesson 31 of your textbook.

Lesson 32

Part 1

a. 2 $\overset{9}{\underline{\quad}}$ 18   b. 5 $\overset{10}{\underline{\quad}}$ 50

_____   _____

_____   _____

Part 2

a. $10 - 5 =$ _____

b. $7 - 5 =$ _____

c. $9 - 5 =$ _____

d. $8 - 5 =$ _____

e. $9 - 5 =$ _____

f. $7 - 5 =$ _____

g. $10 - 5 =$ _____

h. $8 - 5 =$ _____

Part 3   Independent Work

Draw the rectangle. Write the multiplication problem and the whole answer.

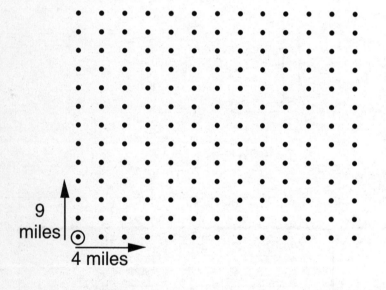

9 miles

4 miles

_____

Part 4   Complete each number family.

a. $\overset{7 \qquad 8}{\longrightarrow}$ ___

b. ___ $\overset{10}{\longrightarrow}$ 13

c. ___ $\overset{7}{\longrightarrow}$ 12

d. $\overset{8}{\underline{\quad}}$ ___ → 16

e. ___ $\overset{9}{\longrightarrow}$ 15

f. $\overset{7 \qquad 7}{\longrightarrow}$ ___

g. $\overset{7}{\underline{\quad}}$ ___ → 15

h. $\overset{6}{\underline{\quad}}$ ___ → 16

i. ___ $\overset{5}{\longrightarrow}$ 9

j. ___ $\overset{6}{\longrightarrow}$ 11

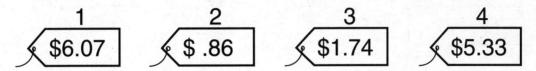

Part 5 A person is not buying all the items that are shown with the price tags. Read each problem to see what the person buys. Add up only those amounts.

a. A person buys items 1, 2 and 4. How much does the person spend?

b. A person buys items 2 and 3. How much does the person spend?

c. A person buys items 1, 2 and 3. How much does the person spend?

Do the independent work for Lesson 32 of your textbook.

Lesson 33

Part 1 For each item circle all the numbers that could be R.

a. $R > 3$ | 20 1 5 2

b. $17 < R$ | 17 21 16 20

c. $100 > R$ | 101 14 17 200

d. $R < 9$ | 9 100 8 11

Part 2 Independent Work

a. $7 - 5 =$ _____

b. $7 - 4 =$ _____

c. $8 - 4 =$ _____

d. $8 - 5 =$ _____

e. $9 - 5 =$ _____

f. $10 - 5 =$ _____

g. $7 - 4 =$ _____

h. $8 - 5 =$ _____

i. $6 - 4 =$ _____

j. $8 - 4 =$ _____

k. $9 - 5 =$ _____

l. $8 - 4 =$ _____

m. $10 - 5 =$ _____

n. $7 - 4 =$ _____

o. $9 - 5 =$ _____

Part 3

Write the multiplication problem and the answer for each rectangle.

a.

7 inches

2 inches

_____

c.

9 inches

5 inches

_____

b.

10 inches

8 inches

_____

Part 4

a. 879
  −788

b. 964
  −245

c. 524
  −194

d. 856
  −609

Part 5

a. 278
  +587

b. 249
  +687

c. 14
   62
  +21

d. 56
   81
  +24

Do the independent work for Lesson 33 of your textbook.

Lesson 34

Part 1

a. $1 \overset{4}{\overline{}}$ ____

b. $1 \overset{7}{\overline{}}$ ____

c. $3 \overset{10}{\overline{}}$ ____

d. $8 \overset{10}{\overline{}}$ ____

e. $1 \overset{10}{\overline{}}$ ____

f. $1 \overset{3}{\overline{}}$ ____

g. $1 \overset{5}{\overline{}}$ ____

h. $4 \overset{10}{\overline{}}$ ____

i. $10 \overset{10}{\overline{}}$ ____

Part 2

a. $7 - 4 =$ ____

b. $10 - 5 =$ ____

c. $8 - 4 =$ ____

d. $9 - 5 =$ ____

e. $8 - 5 =$ ____

f. $7 - 4 =$ ____

g. $8 - 5 =$ ____

h. $7 - 5 =$ ____

i. $8 - 4 =$ ____

j. $9 - 5 =$ ____

k. $10 - 5 =$ ____

l. $7 - 4 =$ ____

m. $8 - 5 =$ ____

n. $9 - 5 =$ ____

o. $8 - 4 =$ ____

Part 3   Independent Work

This table shows the miles each person walked on 3 different days.
Fill in the totals. Then answer each question.

a. The fewest miles were walked on which day? _____

b. Who walked the most total miles? _____

c. Who walked the fewest miles on Sunday? _____

d. The most miles were walked on which day? _____

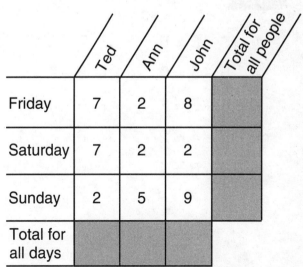

	Ted	Ann	John	Total for all people
Friday	7	2	8	
Saturday	7	2	2	
Sunday	2	5	9	
Total for all days				

a.
```
   14
  177
+  72
```

b.
```
  743
+ 194
```

c.
```
  134
+  95
```

d.
```
  933
  472
+   9
```

Part 5 Write the multiplication problem and the whole answer for each rectangle.

a. 2 feet

9
feet

b. 5 feet

7
feet

Lesson 35

Part 1

a. 10 − 5 = **5**

b. 7 − 5 = **2**

c. 9 − 5 = **4**

d. 6 − 5 = **1**

e. 5 − 5 = **0**

f. 9 − 5 = **4**

g. 7 − 5 = **2**

h. 10 − 5 = **5**

i. 8 − 5 = **3**

j. 8 − 4 = **4**

k. 7 − 4 = **3**

l. 7 − 5 = **2**

m. 6 − 4 = **2**

n. 6 − 5 = **1**

o. 7 − 5 = **2**

p. 9 − 5 = **4**

q. 10 − 5 = **5**

a. 1 $\overset{5}{\overline{}}$ ___   b. 1 $\overset{9}{\overline{}}$ ___   c. 5 $\overset{10}{\overline{}}$ ___   d. 9 $\overset{10}{\overline{}}$ ___

e. 1 $\overset{7}{\overline{}}$ ___   f. 6 $\overset{10}{\overline{}}$ ___   g. 1 $\overset{10}{\overline{}}$ ___   h. 10 $\overset{10}{\overline{}}$ ___

i. 2 $\overset{10}{\overline{}}$ ___   j. 1 $\overset{3}{\overline{}}$ ___

Part 3 — Independent Work

For each item, write the column problem and figure out the answer.

a. Debbie started with 748 baseball cards. She traded away 592 cards. How many baseball cards did she end up with?

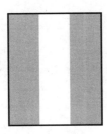

b. Joe had $2.53. He earned $7.93. How much did he end up with?

c. A farmer had 288 eggs. He sold 149 eggs. How many eggs did the farmer end up with?

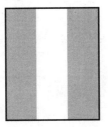

Part 4

a. 643 — 634   b. 945 — 95   c. 99 — 100   d. 599 — 500

Part 5

a. 429
   +395

b. 194
   +578

c. 234
   +765

d. 456
   +987

Lesson 36

Part 1

a. $3 \longrightarrow 7$ b. $4 \longrightarrow 8$ c. $3 \longrightarrow 8$ d. $4 \longrightarrow 9$

Part 2

a. $4 \longrightarrow 9$ b. $4 \longrightarrow 8$ c. $3 \longrightarrow 8$ d. $3 \longrightarrow 7$

e. $4 \longrightarrow 9$ f. $3 \longrightarrow 8$ g. $4 \longrightarrow 9$ h. $4 \longrightarrow 8$

i. $3 \longrightarrow 7$ j. $4 \longrightarrow 8$ k. $3 \longrightarrow 8$ l. $4 \longrightarrow 9$

Part 3

a. $4 \overset{10}{\longrightarrow}$ ___   b. $2 \overset{10}{\longrightarrow}$ ___   c. $9 \overset{10}{\longrightarrow}$ ___   d. $10 \overset{10}{\longrightarrow}$ ___

e. $1 \overset{10}{\longrightarrow}$ ___   f. $1 \overset{6}{\longrightarrow}$ ___   g. $1 \overset{2}{\longrightarrow}$ ___   h. $1 \overset{1}{\longrightarrow}$ ___

Part 4   **Independent Work**

A person is not buying all the items that are shown with the price tags.
Read each problem to see what the person buys.
Add up only those amounts.

| 1 | 2 | 3 | 4 |
| $9.46 | $1.65 | $8.09 | $ .06 |

a. A person buys items 1, 2 and 4. How much does the person spend?

b. A person buys items 2, 3 and 4. How much does the person spend?

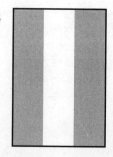

Do the independent work for Lesson 36 of your textbook.

64

Lesson 37

Part 1

a. 3 ⟶ 8   b. 3 ⟶ 7   c. 4 ⟶ 8   d. 4 ⟶ 9

e. 3 ⟶ 7   f. 4 ⟶ 8   g. 4 ⟶ 9   h. 3 ⟶ 8

Part 2

a. You have 2 tens.

b. You have 2 sevens.

c. You have 2 fives.

d. You have 2 threes.

e. You have 2 nines.

Part 3

a. 8 $\overset{5}{\cancel{6}}$ ^{1}3

b. 7 $\overset{3}{\cancel{4}}$ ^{1}5

c. 2 $\overset{8}{\cancel{9}}$ ^{1}7

d. 3 $\overset{5}{\cancel{6}}$ ^{1}0

Part 4   Independent Work

Complete each number family.

a. 7 ⟶ 16   b. 7   8 ⟶ __   c. 4 ⟶ 9   d. __ 10 ⟶ 14

e. 4 ⟶ 13   f. __ 9 ⟶ 16   g. 8   8 ⟶ __   h. 8   7 ⟶ __

i. 1 ⟶ 11   j. __ 5 ⟶ 8   k. 9 ⟶ 16   l. 8 ⟶ 15

Do the independent work for Lesson 37 of your textbook.

Lesson 38

Part 1

a. $1 \times 6 =$ _____ b. $1 \times 4 =$ _____ c. $4 \times 10 =$ _____ d. $8 \times 10 =$ _____

e. $2 \times 10 =$ _____ f. $1 \times 3 =$ _____ g. $1 \times 1 =$ _____ h. $10 \times 10 =$ _____

i. $1 \times 2 =$ _____ j. $5 \times 10 =$ _____

Part 2

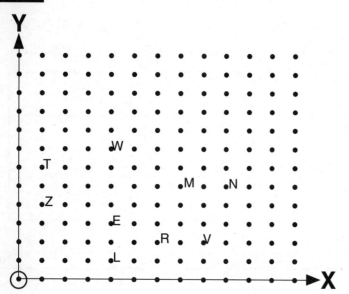

a. $(X = 4, Y = 3)$

b. $(X = 6, Y = 2)$

c. $(X = 1, Y = 4)$

d. $(X = 7, Y = 5)$

Part 3

a. $5\overset{6}{7}8$ b. $7\overset{8}{9}\overset{1}{2}$

c. $4\overset{1}{2}0$ d. $8\overset{0}{7}\overset{1}{1}$

Part 4

a. $\begin{array}{r} 644 \\ -499 \\ \hline \end{array}$ b. $\begin{array}{r} 767 \\ -498 \\ \hline \end{array}$ c. $\begin{array}{r} 463 \\ -369 \\ \hline \end{array}$

Part 5   **Independent Work**

a. $7 - 3 =$ _____ b. $8 - 4 =$ _____ c. $8 - 3 =$ _____ d. $9 - 4 =$ _____

e. $8 - 4 =$ _____ f. $9 - 4 =$ _____ g. $7 - 3 =$ _____ h. $8 - 3 =$ _____

i. $8 - 3 =$ _____ j. $7 - 3 =$ _____ k. $9 - 4 =$ _____ l. $8 - 4 =$ _____

Do the independent work for Lesson 38 of your textbook.

Lesson 39

a. $4 \times 10 =$ _____   b. $10 \times 6 =$ _____   c. $5 \times 1 =$ _____   d. $7 \times 1 =$ _____

e. $3 \times 1 =$ _____   f. $3 \times 10 =$ _____   g. $8 \times 1 =$ _____   h. $10 \times 9 =$ _____

i. $1 \times 6 =$ _____   j. $10 \times 4 =$ _____

Part 2

a. $7 - 3 =$ _____   b. $8 - 3 =$ _____   c. $8 - 4 =$ _____   d. $9 - 4 =$ _____

e. $8 - 3 =$ _____   f. $9 - 4 =$ _____   g. $7 - 3 =$ _____   h. $8 - 4 =$ _____

i. $7 - 3 =$ _____   j. $8 - 4 =$ _____   k. $9 - 4 =$ _____   l. $8 - 3 =$ _____

Part 3

a.
$$\begin{array}{r} 460 \\ -369 \\ \hline \end{array}$$

b.
$$\begin{array}{r} 613 \\ -\ \ 94 \\ \hline \end{array}$$

c.
$$\begin{array}{r} 248 \\ -149 \\ \hline \end{array}$$

Part 4   **Independent Work**

This table shows the hours people worked on three different days.

a. Who worked the most hours?

_____

b. On which day were the fewest hours worked? _____

c. Who worked the most hours on Thursday? _____

d. Who worked the fewest total hours?

_____

e. On which day were the most hours worked? _____

	Karen	Susie	Brent	Total for all days
Tuesday	2	8	7	
Thursday	11	1	1	
Friday	7	3	9	
Total for all people				

Do the independent work for Lesson 39 of your textbook.

Lesson 40

a. 951
-452

b. 793
-299

c. 347
-249

Part 2 Independent Work

For each item, circle all the numbers that could be the letter.

a. $4000 \angle N$ | 401   99   787   5000 |

b. $650 \angle R$ | 99   689   652   650 |

c. $T \searrow 0$ | 5   0   10   975 |

Part 3 Draw the rectangle. Write the area problem and the whole answer.

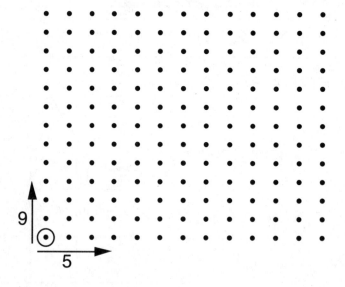

_____

Do the independent work for Lesson 40 of your textbook.

Test 4

Part 1

a. 1 $\xrightarrow{5}$ ____   b. 10 $\xrightarrow{10}$ ____   c. 4 $\xrightarrow{10}$ ____   d. 1 $\xrightarrow{7}$ ____

e. 10 $\xrightarrow{3}$ ____   f. 8 $\xrightarrow{1}$ ____   g. 1 $\xrightarrow{9}$ ____   h. 2 $\xrightarrow{10}$ ____

i. 7 $\xrightarrow{10}$ ____   j. 6 $\xrightarrow{1}$ ____   k. 10 $\xrightarrow{8}$ ____   l. 3 $\xrightarrow{1}$ ____

Part 2

a. $8 - 3 =$ ____   b. $7 - 3 =$ ____   c. $8 - 4 =$ ____   d. $9 - 4 =$ ____

e. $9 - 3 =$ ____   f. $7 - 1 =$ ____   g. $7 - 3 =$ ____   h. $5 - 1 =$ ____

i. $7 - 3 =$ ____   j. $9 - 1 =$ ____   k. $7 - 4 =$ ____   l. $8 - 1 =$ ____

Part 3

a.
$$\begin{array}{r} 264 \\ -\ 95 \\ \hline \end{array}$$

b.
$$\begin{array}{r} 884 \\ -785 \\ \hline \end{array}$$

c.
$$\begin{array}{r} 487 \\ -399 \\ \hline \end{array}$$

d.
$$\begin{array}{r} 586 \\ -487 \\ \hline \end{array}$$

Part 4 Write the numeral for each item.

a. Seven thousand four.

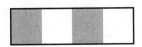

b. Seven hundred four.

c. Four thousand twenty.

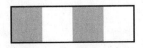

Part 5 Write the letter shown on the grid for each item.

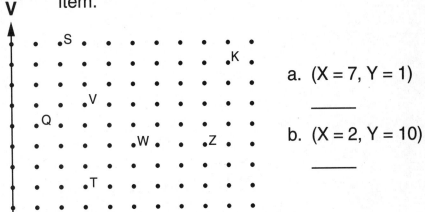

a. $(X = 7, Y = 1)$

____

b. $(X = 2, Y = 10)$

____

Go to Test 4 in your textbook.

69

Start

Test Lesson 4

Fact Game 1

$1+1=2$ $2+1=3$ $1+3=4$ $4+1=5$ $1+5=6$ $6+1=7$ $1+7=8$ $8+1=9$ $1+9=10$ $10+1=11$

$2+2=4$ $3+2=5$ $2+4=6$ $5+2=7$ $2+6=8$ $7+2=9$ $2+8=10$ $9+2=11$ $2+10=12$

$3+3=6$ $4+3=7$ $3+5=8$ $6+3=9$ $3+7=10$ $8+3=11$ $3+9=12$ $10+3=13$

$4+4=8$ $5+4=9$ $4+6=10$ $7+4=11$ $4+8=12$ $9+4=13$ $4+10=14$

$5+5=10$ $6+5=11$ $5+7=12$ $8+5=13$ $5+9=14$ $10+5=15$

$6+6=12$ $7+6=13$ $6+8=14$ $9+6=15$ $6+10=16$

$7+7=14$ $8+7=15$ $7+9=16$ $10+7=17$

$8+8=16$ $9+8=17$ $8+10=18$

$9+9=18$ $10+9=19$

Finish $10+10=20$

Start

Test Lesson 4

Fact Game 2

$2-1=1$ $3-1=2$ $4-1=3$ $5-1=4$ $6-1=5$ $7-1=6$ $8-1=7$ $9-1=8$ $10-9=1$ $11-10=1$

$4-2=2$ $5-2=3$ $6-2=4$ $7-2=5$ $8-2=6$ $9-2=7$ $10-2=8$ $11-9=2$ $12-10=2$

$7-3=4$ $8-3=5$ $12-9=3$ $13-10=3$

$8-4=4$ $9-4=5$ $13-9=4$ $14-10=4$

$10-5=5$ $14-9=5$ $15-10=5$

$15-9=6$ $16-10=6$

$16-9=7$ $17-10=7$

$17-9=8$ $18-10=8$

$18-9=9$ $19-10=9$

Finish $20-10=10$

70

Test 4/Extra Practice

a. 4 | 10 → ____   b. 2 | 10 → ____   c. 9 | 10 → ____   d. 10 | 10 → ____

e. 1 | 10 → ____   f. 1 | 6 → ____   g. 1 | 2 → ____   h. 1 | 1 → ____

Part 2

a. 7 − 3 = ____   b. 8 − 3 = ____   c. 8 − 4 = ____   d. 9 − 4 = ____

e. 8 − 3 = ____   f. 9 − 4 = ____   g. 7 − 3 = ____   h. 8 − 4 = ____

i. 7 − 3 = ____   j. 8 − 4 = ____   k. 9 − 4 = ____   l. 8 − 3 = ____

Part 3

a. 644
  − 499

b. 767
  − 498

c. 463
  − 369

Lesson 41

a. 2 ⌐→ 7 ____   b. 2 ⌐→ 4 ____   c. 2 ⌐→ 6 ____   d. 2 ⌐→ 8 ____

e. 2 ⌐→ 9 ____   f. 2 ⌐→ 5 ____   g. 2 ⌐→ 3 ____   h. 2 ⌐→ 2 ____

i. 2 ⌐→ 10 ____

Part 2

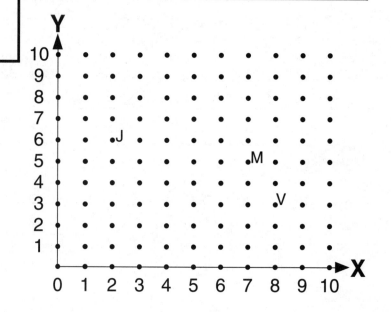

a. Letter J.   (X = ____, Y = ____)

b. Letter M.   (X = ____, Y = ____)

c. Letter V.   (X = ____, Y = ____)

Part 3

a. 4 ⟹ 8   4 ⟹ 9   4 ⟹ 10   4 ⟹ 11   4 ⟹ 12

b. 4 ⟹ 10   4 ⟹ 8   4 ⟹ 12   4 ⟹ 9   4 ⟹ 11

c. 4 ⟹ 12   4 ⟹ 10   4 ⟹ 8   4 ⟹ 11   4 ⟹ 9

____   ____   ____   ____   ____

Part 4

a. 469
   −276

b. 496
   −297

c. 741
   −509

d. 734
   −299

Lesson 42

Part 1

a. Letter A.   (X = _____, Y = _____)

b. Letter B.   (X = _____, Y = _____)

c. Letter C.   (X = _____, Y = _____)

Part 2

a.
$$\begin{array}{r} 568 \\ -457 \\ \hline \end{array}$$

b.
$$\begin{array}{r} 557 \\ -458 \\ \hline \end{array}$$

c.
$$\begin{array}{r} 908 \\ -310 \\ \hline \end{array}$$

d.
$$\begin{array}{r} 678 \\ -409 \\ \hline \end{array}$$

e.
$$\begin{array}{r} 843 \\ -199 \\ \hline \end{array}$$

Part 3

a. 2 ⟶ 6 _____

b. 2 ⟶ 9 _____

c. 2 ⟶ 4 _____

d. 2 ⟶ 2 _____

e. 2 ⟶ 5 _____

f. 2 ⟶ 3 _____

g. 2 ⟶ 7 _____

h. 2 ⟶ 8 _____

Part 4

a. 4 ⟶ 9

b. 4 ⟶ 10

c. 4 ⟶ 11

d. 4 ⟶ 12

e. 4 ⟶ 11

f. 4 ⟶ 9

g. 4 ⟶ 12

h. 4 ⟶ 10

i. 4 ⟶ 12

j. 4 ⟶ 10

k. 4 ⟶ 9

l. 4 ⟶ 11

Lesson 43

a. $\dfrac{4}{\longrightarrow}$ 13   e. $\dfrac{4}{\longrightarrow}$ 9

b. $\dfrac{4}{\longrightarrow}$ 10   f. $\dfrac{4}{\longrightarrow}$ 12

c. $\dfrac{4}{\longrightarrow}$ 12   g. $\dfrac{4}{\longrightarrow}$ 10

d. $\dfrac{4}{\longrightarrow}$ 11   h. $\dfrac{4}{\longrightarrow}$ 11

_____

_____

_____

_____

Part 2

a. $2\overline{\smash{\big)}\,}$ $\overset{4}{\longrightarrow}$ ____   b. $2\overline{\smash{\big)}\,}$ $\overset{7}{\longrightarrow}$ ____   c. $2\overline{\smash{\big)}\,}$ $\overset{5}{\longrightarrow}$ ____   d. $2\overline{\smash{\big)}\,}$ $\overset{9}{\longrightarrow}$ ____

e. $2\overline{\smash{\big)}\,}$ $\overset{6}{\longrightarrow}$ ____   f. $2\overline{\smash{\big)}\,}$ $\overset{8}{\longrightarrow}$ ____   g. $2\overline{\smash{\big)}\,}$ $\overset{10}{\longrightarrow}$ ____

Part 3 — Independent Work

Draw the rectangle. Write the multiplication problem and the whole answer.

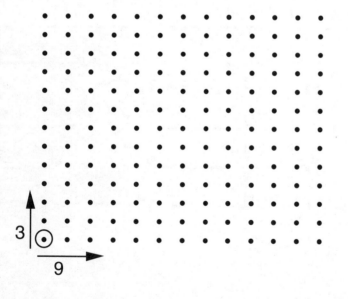

3
9

Part 4

a. $8 - 5 = $ ____

b. $9 - 4 = $ ____

c. $7 - 4 = $ ____

d. $10 - 5 = $ ____

e. $8 - 4 = $ ____

f. $6 - 2 = $ ____

g. $9 - 5 = $ ____

h. $6 - 4 = $ ____

i. $9 - 4 = $ ____

j. $7 - 2 = $ ____

Do the independent work for Lesson 43 of your textbook.

Lesson 44

Part 1

a. You have   or   You have
    4 twos.   2 fours.

b. You have   or   You have
    5 twos.   2 fives.

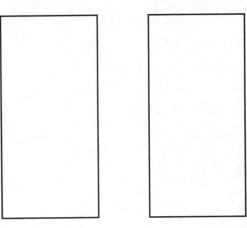

Part 2

a. $2 \times 6 = \underline{\hphantom{00}}$ b. $2 \times 4 = \underline{\hphantom{00}}$ c. $2 \times 5 = \underline{\hphantom{00}}$

d. $2 \times 7 = \underline{\hphantom{00}}$ e. $2 \times 8 = \underline{\hphantom{00}}$ f. $2 \times 9 = \underline{\hphantom{00}}$

g. $2 \times 2 = \underline{\hphantom{00}}$ h. $2 \times 3 = \underline{\hphantom{00}}$ i. $2 \times 1 = \underline{\hphantom{00}}$

Part 3

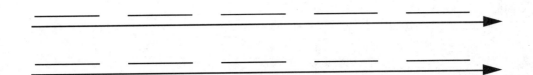

Part 4

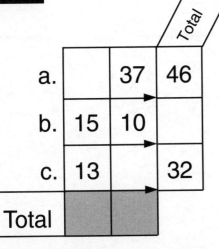

a.   b.   c.

Lesson 45

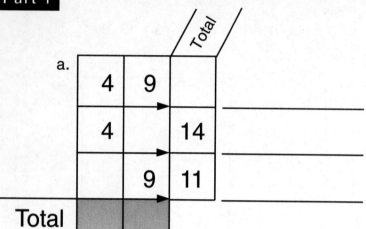

a.

		Total
4	9	
4		14
	9	11
Total		

b.

		Total
9		13
	4	10
3	8	
Total		

Part 2

a. $11 - 4 =$ _____   b. $12 - 4 =$ _____   c. $10 - 4 =$ _____

d. $9 - 4 =$ _____   e. $10 - 4 =$ _____   f. $13 - 4 =$ _____

g. $12 - 4 =$ _____   h. $11 - 4 =$ _____

Part 3

a. $2 \times 9 =$ _____   b. $2 \times 6 =$ _____   c. $2 \times 4 =$ _____

d. $2 \times 8 =$ _____   e. $2 \times 10 =$ _____   f. $2 \times 7 =$ _____

g. $2 \times 5 =$ _____   h. $2 \times 3 =$ _____

Lesson 46

Part 1

a. $6 \times 2 =$ _____

b. $4 \times 2 =$ _____

c. $7 \times 2 =$ _____

d. $2 \times 2 =$ _____

e. $2 \times 9 =$ _____

f. $2 \times 5 =$ _____

g. $8 \times 2 =$ _____

h. $2 \times 6 =$ _____

i. $2 \times 8 =$ _____

j. $2 \times 10 =$ _____

k. $9 \times 2 =$ _____

l. $2 \times 9 =$ _____

Part 2

a. 5 tens

b. 17 tens

c. 23 tens

d. 7 tens

e. 12 tens

f. 2 tens

g. 42 tens

Part 3

a. $14 - 4 =$ _____

b. $13 - 4 =$ _____

c. $12 - 4 =$ _____

d. $11 - 4 =$ _____

d. $10 - 4 =$ _____

f. $12 - 4 =$ _____

g. $10 - 4 =$ _____

h. $8 - 4 =$ _____

i. $11 - 4 =$ _____

j. $13 - 4 =$ _____

Part 4

a.
$$5 \quad\quad 35$$
$$+4 \quad + 4$$

b.
$$3 \quad\quad 53$$
$$+3 \quad + 3$$

c.
$$3 \quad\quad 83$$
$$+6 \quad + 6$$

d.
$$2 \quad\quad 72$$
$$+4 \quad + 4$$

e.
$$4 \quad\quad 64$$
$$+4 \quad + 4$$

Part 5

Do the independent work for Lesson 46 of your textbook.

Lesson 47

a. $6 \times 2 =$ _____   b. $9 \times 2 =$ _____   c. $7 \times 2 =$ _____   d. $4 \times 2 =$ _____

e. $2 \times 8 =$ _____   f. $2 \times 5 =$ _____   g. $2 \times 3 =$ _____   h. $10 \times 2 =$ _____

i. $3 \times 2 =$ _____   j. $2 \times 7 =$ _____   k. $5 \times 2 =$ _____   l. $8 \times 2 =$ _____

Part 2

hundreds / tens / ones

a. 19 tens

b. 54 tens

c. 29 tens

d. 4 tens

e. 74 tens

Part 3

a. $\begin{array}{r} 4 \\ +3 \\ \hline \end{array}$ $\begin{array}{r} 74 \\ +\ 3 \\ \hline \end{array}$ b. $\begin{array}{r} 6 \\ +3 \\ \hline \end{array}$ $\begin{array}{r} 16 \\ +\ 3 \\ \hline \end{array}$

c. $\begin{array}{r} 2 \\ +5 \\ \hline \end{array}$ $\begin{array}{r} 62 \\ +\ 5 \\ \hline \end{array}$ d. $\begin{array}{r} 3 \\ +5 \\ \hline \end{array}$ $\begin{array}{r} 33 \\ +\ 5 \\ \hline \end{array}$

Part 4   **Independent Work**

a. $7 - 5 =$ _____   b. $7 - 4 =$ _____   c. $9 - 2 =$ _____   d. $8 - 4 =$ _____

e. $10 - 9 =$ _____   f. $7 - 6 =$ _____   g. $8 - 4 =$ _____   h. $6 - 2 =$ _____

i. $7 - 4 =$ _____   j. $9 - 1 =$ _____   k. $7 - 4 =$ _____   l. $3 - 1 =$ _____

m. $7 - 5 =$ _____   n. $8 - 4 =$ _____   o. $6 - 2 =$ _____   p. $6 - 1 =$ _____

Do the independent work for Lesson 47 of your textbook.

Lesson 48

Part 1

a. $12 - 4 = $ ____   b. $7 - 2 = $ ____   c. $7 - 4 = $ ____   d. $7 - 3 = $ ____

e. $9 - 4 = $ ____   f. $9 - 7 = $ ____   g. $13 - 4 = $ ____   h. $8 - 4 = $ ____

i. $8 - 3 = $ ____   j. $8 - 8 = $ ____   k. $6 - 4 = $ ____   l. $14 - 4 = $ ____

m. $14 - 5 = $ ____   n. $5 - 5 = $ ____   o. $14 - 0 = $ ____

Part 2

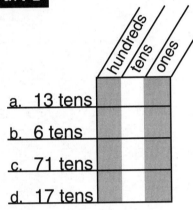

a. 13 tens

b. 6 tens

c. 71 tens

d. 17 tens

Part 3

a.
$$6 \quad 36$$
$$+2 \quad +\ 2$$

b.
$$1 \quad 51$$
$$+4 \quad +\ 4$$

c.
$$3 \quad 23$$
$$+5 \quad +\ 5$$

d.
$$2 \quad 82$$
$$+7 \quad +\ 7$$

Part 4 — Independent Work

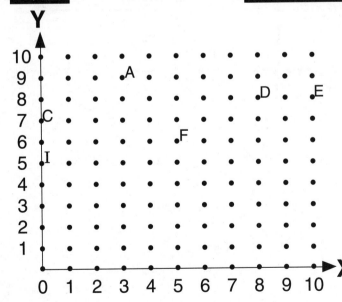

Write the letter for each description.

- Letter ____ (X = 10, Y = 8)

- Letter ____ (X = 0, Y = 7)

- Letter ____ (X = 5, Y = 6)

Write the X and Y values.

- Letter A. (X = ____, Y = ____)

- Letter D. (X = ____, Y = ____)

- Letter I. (X = ____, Y = ____)

Do the independent work for Lesson 48 of your textbook.

Lesson 49

Part 1

a. 12 − 4 = _____   b. 10 − 4 = _____   c. 11 − 7 = _____   d. 12 − 9 = _____

e. 12 − 8 = _____   f. 9 − 5 = _____   g. 10 − 5 = _____   h. 13 − 4 = _____

i. 11 − 4 = _____   j. 10 − 4 = _____   k. 10 − 6 = _____   l. 10 − 8 = _____

Part 2

a. 3$\underline{6}$ + $\underline{2}$ = _____   b. 3$\underline{4}$ + $\underline{5}$ = _____   c. 8$\underline{3}$ + $\underline{2}$ = _____   d. 5$\underline{1}$ + $\underline{6}$ = _____

Part 3

a. 3 ⌐→ 4 → _____

b. 1 ⌐→ 4 → _____

_____

c. 4 ⌐→ 4 → _____

d. 2 ⌐→ 4 → _____

_____

Part 4

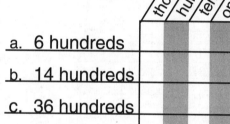

	thousands	hundreds	tens	ones
a. 6 hundreds				
b. 14 hundreds				
c. 36 hundreds				
d. 12 hundreds				
e. 9 hundreds				

Part 5   Independent Work

a. 5 x 10 = _____   b. 10 x 4 = _____   c. 2 x 6 = _____   d.   5 x 2 = _____

e. 7 x 10 = _____   f. 2 x 2 = _____   g. 7 x 2 = _____   h.   2 x 3 = _____

i. 10 x 9 = _____   j. 2 x 5 = _____   k. 10 x 3 = _____   l. 10 x 10 = _____

m. 2 x 4 = _____   n. 8 x 10 = _____   o. 3 x 2 = _____

Do the independent work for Lesson 49 of your textbook.

Lesson 50

Part 1

a. 10 − 4 = _____   b.   10 − 6 = _____   c. 10 − 8 = _____   d.   10 − 9 = _____

e. 12 − 8 = _____   f. 12 − 10 = _____   g. 11 − 7 = _____   h.   12 − 4 = _____

i. 13 − 9 = _____   j.   11 − 4 = _____   k. 13 − 4 = _____   l. 14 − 10 = _____

m. 10 − 6 = _____   n.   11 − 7 = _____   o. 12 − 8 = _____

Part 2

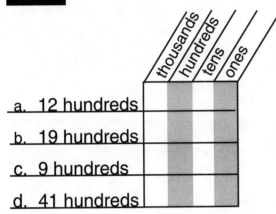

a. 12 hundreds

b. 19 hundreds

c. 9 hundreds

d. 41 hundreds

Part 3

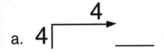

a. 4 ⌐→ 4 _____   b. 2 ⌐→ 4 _____

_____   _____

c. 1 ⌐→ 4 _____   d. 3 ⌐→ 4 _____

_____   _____

Part 4

a. 2$\underline{5}$ + $\underline{3}$ = _____   b. 7$\underline{4}$ + $\underline{1}$ = _____   c. 8$\underline{3}$ + $\underline{6}$ = _____   d. 4$\underline{4}$ + $\underline{5}$ = _____

Part 5

a. 2 x 5 = _____   b.   1 x 7 = _____   c. 8 x 10 = _____   d.   3 x 2 = _____

e. 7 x 2 = _____   f. 7 x 10 = _____   g. 7 x 1 = _____   h.   5 x 2 = _____

i. 5 x 10 = _____   j.   5 x 1 = _____   k. 8 x 2 = _____   l. 10 x 8 = _____

Test 5

a. 10 − 4 = _____   b.   10 − 6 = _____   c.   10 − 8 = _____   d.   10 − 9 = _____

e. 12 − 8 = _____   f.   12 − 10 = _____   g.   11 − 7 = _____   h.   12 − 4 = _____

i. 13 − 9 = _____   j.   11 − 4 = _____   k.   13 − 4 = _____   l. 14 − 10 = _____

Part 2

a.   2   b. 1   c.   8   d.   3
   x 5   x 7   x 10   x 2

e.   7   f.   7   g.   7   h.   5
   x 2   x 10   x 1   x 2

i.   5   j. 5   k.   8   l. 10
   x 10   x 1   x 2   x 8

Part 5 Write the complete number family. Then write the addition problem or subtraction problem and the answer. Remember the unit name.

a. Debby was 21 inches taller than Billy. Billy was 37 inches tall. How tall was Debby?

b. Reggie was 17 inches shorter than Billy. Billy was 37 inches tall. How tall was Reggie?

Part 3 Write each numeral.

a. 6 hundreds

b. 14 hundreds

Part 4 Write both multiplication facts for each family.

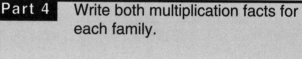

a. 9 |‾10‾→ _____

_____

_____

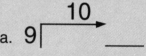

b. 1 |‾7‾→ _____

_____

_____

Write the X and Y values for each letter.

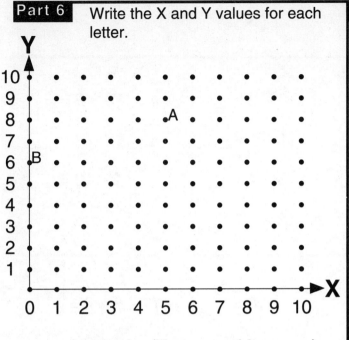

- Letter A. (X = _____, Y = _____)

- Letter B. (X = _____, Y = _____)

Write the problems for each row and the answer. Then write the missing numbers in the table and figure out the total for the two columns.

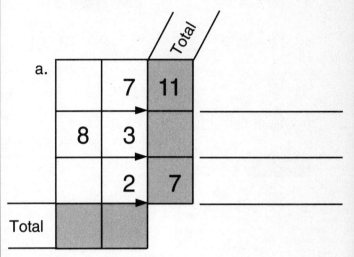

End of Test 5

Test Lesson 5

Fact Game

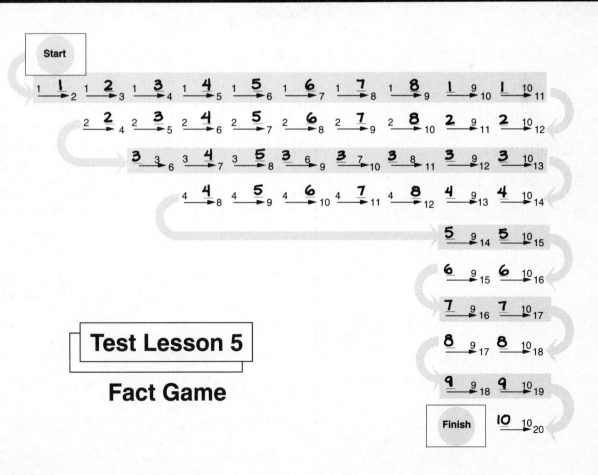

Test 5/Extra Practice

a. 10 − 4 = _____   b.   10 − 6 = _____   c. 10 − 8 = _____   d.   10 − 9 = _____

e. 12 − 8 = _____   f. 12 − 10 = _____   g. 11 − 7 = _____   h.   12 − 4 = _____

i. 13 − 9 = _____   j.   11 − 4 = _____   k. 13 − 4 = _____   l. 14 − 10 = _____

m. 10 − 6 = _____   n.   11 − 7 = _____   o. 12 − 8 = _____

Part 5

a.   2 x 5 = _____   b.   1 x 7 = _____   c. 8 x 10 = _____   d.   3 x 2 = _____

e.   7 x 2 = _____   f. 7 x 10 = _____   g.   7 x 1 = _____   h.   5 x 2 = _____

i. 5 x 10 = _____   j.   5 x 1 = _____   k.   8 x 2 = _____   l. 10 x 8 = _____

m.   8 x 1 = _____

Part 3

	thousands	hundreds	tens	ones
a. 12 hundreds				
b. 19 hundreds				
c. 9 hundreds				
d. 41 hundreds				

Part 4

a. Letter J.   (X = _____, Y = _____)

b. Letter M. (X = _____, Y = _____)

c. Letter V.   (X = _____, Y = _____)

Lesson 51

Part 1

a. $8 - 4 =$ _____   b. $13 - 9 =$ _____   c. $7 - 3 =$ _____   d. $12 - 4 =$ _____

e. $9 - 4 =$ _____   f. $10 - 6 =$ _____   g. $6 - 4 =$ _____   h. $13 - 4 =$ _____

i. $7 - 4 =$ _____   j. $12 - 8 =$ _____   k. $11 - 7 =$ _____   l. $9 - 5 =$ _____

m. $11 - 4 =$ _____   n. $14 - 10 =$ _____   o. $10 - 4 =$ _____   p. $4 - 4 =$ _____

Part 2

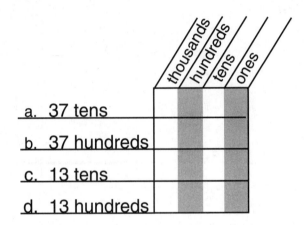

a. 37 tens

b. 37 hundreds

c. 13 tens

d. 13 hundreds

Part 3

a. $35 + 2 =$ _____   c. $53 + 5 =$ _____

b. $64 + 4 =$ _____   d. $42 + 6 =$ _____

Part 4

a. $1 \times 4 =$ _____   e. $3 \times 4 =$ _____

b. $3 \times 4 =$ _____   f. $1 \times 4 =$ _____

c. $2 \times 4 =$ _____   g. $4 \times 4 =$ _____

d. $4 \times 4 =$ _____   h. $2 \times 4 =$ _____

Part 5   Independent Work

a. $10 \times 3 =$ _____   b. $2 \times 8 =$ _____   c. $6 \times 2 =$ _____   d. $5 \times 1 =$ _____

e. $7 \times 2 =$ _____   f. $10 \times 3 =$ _____   g. $2 \times 6 =$ _____   h. $9 \times 2 =$ _____

i. $2 \times 7 =$ _____   j. $1 \times 6 =$ _____   k. $8 \times 2 =$ _____   l. $10 \times 4 =$ _____

m. $5 \times 2 =$ _____   n. $2 \times 9 =$ _____

Lesson 52

a. 4	b. 4	c. 4	d. 4	e. 2	f. 2	g. 3	h. 1
x 3	x 2	x 1	x 4	x 4	x 8	x 4	x 4

i. 6	j. 3	k. 3	l. 2	m. 4	n. 2	o. 2	p. 1
x 2	x 2	x 4	x 4	x 4	x 3	x 9	x 4

Part 2

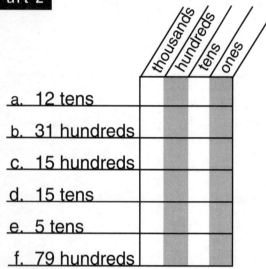

a. 12 tens

b. 31 hundreds

c. 15 hundreds

d. 15 tens

e. 5 tens

f. 79 hundreds

Part 3

a. 71 + 5 = _____

b. 26 + 3 = _____

c. 82 + 7 = _____

d. 43 + 3 = _____

e. 23 + 5 = _____

Part 5   Independent Work

Write the number problem and the answer for each row. Then write the missing numbers in the table and figure out the total for the two columns.

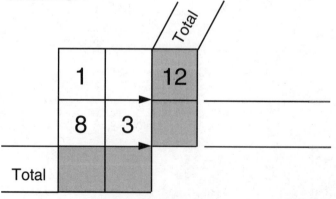

Part 4

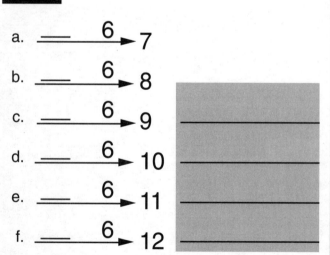

a. ═══ 6 → 7

b. ═══ 6 → 8

c. ═══ 6 → 9

d. ═══ 6 → 10

e. ═══ 6 → 11

f. ═══ 6 → 12

Lesson 53

a. ══ $\xrightarrow{6}$ 9   e. ══ $\xrightarrow{6}$ 10   i. ══ $\xrightarrow{6}$ 12

b. ══ $\xrightarrow{6}$ 10   f. ══ $\xrightarrow{6}$ 12   j. ══ $\xrightarrow{6}$ 9

c. ══ $\xrightarrow{6}$ 11   g. ══ $\xrightarrow{6}$ 9   k. ══ $\xrightarrow{6}$ 11

d. ══ $\xrightarrow{6}$ 12   h. ══ $\xrightarrow{6}$ 11   l. ══ $\xrightarrow{6}$ 10

Part 2

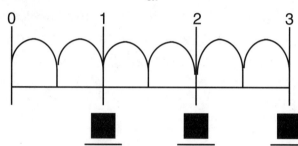

a.

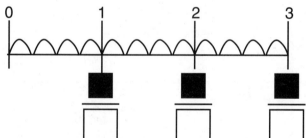

b.

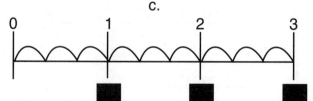

c.

Part 3

a. $4 \times 3 =$ ____   g. $2 \times 7 =$ ____

b. $4 \times 1 =$ ____   h. $4 \times 4 =$ ____

c. $2 \times 6 =$ ____   i. $3 \times 4 =$ ____

d. $2 \times 9 =$ ____   j. $4 \times 2 =$ ____

e. $2 \times 5 =$ ____   k. $6 \times 2 =$ ____

f. $4 \times 5 =$ ____   l. $2 \times 8 =$ ____

Part 4

a. $55 + 3 =$ ____   d. $94 + 4 =$ ____

b. $27 + 2 =$ ____   e. $23 + 2 =$ ____

c. $82 + 6 =$ ____

Lesson 54

Part 1

a. ══ →6→ 11

b. ══ →6→ 9

c. ══ →6→ 12

d. ══ →6→ 10

e. ══ →6→ 9

f. ══ →6→ 11

g. ══ →6→ 12

h. ══ →6→ 10

i. ══ →6→ 10

j. ══ →6→ 12

k. ══ →6→ 9

l. ══ →6→ 11

Part 2

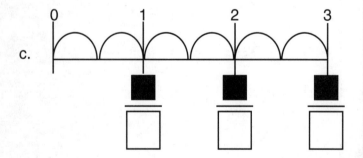

Part 3   Independent Work

Figure out the missing numbers in the table. Start with any row or column that has two numbers.

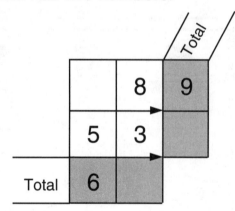

		Total
	8	9
5	3	
Total 6		

Part 4

	thousands	hundreds	tens	ones
a. 56 hundreds				
b. 65 tens				
c. 35 ones				
d. 34 hundreds				
e. 7 tens				
f. 79 hundreds				

88

Lesson 55

Part 1

a. $2\overline{\smash{\big)}}^{5\rightarrow}$ _____ _____

b. $5\overline{\smash{\big)}}^{5\rightarrow}$ _____ _____

c. $3\overline{\smash{\big)}}^{5\rightarrow}$ _____ _____

d. $1\overline{\smash{\big)}}^{5\rightarrow}$ _____ _____

e. $4\overline{\smash{\big)}}^{5\rightarrow}$ _____ _____

Part 2

a.

b.

c.

Part 3

a. $10 - 6 =$ _____   e. $9 - 6 =$ _____

b. $12 - 6 =$ _____   f. $11 - 6 =$ _____

c. $9 - 6 =$ _____   g. $10 - 6 =$ _____

d. $11 - 6 =$ _____   h. $11 - 6 =$ _____

Part 4 — Independent Work

Write the X and Y values for each letter.

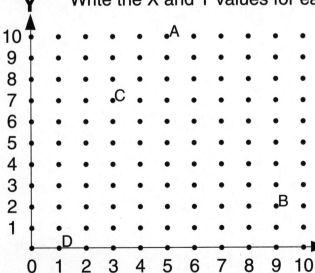

- Letter A. ($X =$ _____, $Y =$ _____)

- Letter B. ($X =$ _____, $Y =$ _____)

- Letter C. ($X =$ _____, $Y =$ _____)

- Letter D. ($X =$ _____, $Y =$ _____)

Lesson 56

Part 1

a. 4 ⌐→ 5 _____ _____

b. 1 ⌐→ 5 _____ _____

c. 3 ⌐→ 5 _____ _____

d. 5 ⌐→ 5 _____ _____

e. 2 ⌐→ 5 _____ _____

Part 2

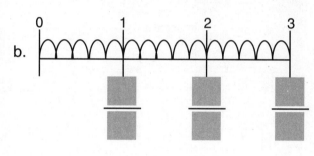

Part 3

a. $11 - 6 =$ _____   b. $9 - 6 =$ _____   c. $12 - 6 =$ _____   d. $10 - 6 =$ _____

e. $12 - 6 =$ _____   f. $10 - 6 =$ _____   g. $9 - 6 =$ _____   h. $11 - 6 =$ _____

Part 4   Independent Work

Write the missing letter for the X and Y values.
Write the missing X and Y values for each letter.

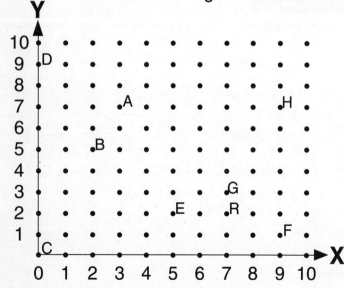

- Letter _____ (X = 7, Y = 3)

- Letter _____ (X = 0, Y = 0)

- Letter _____ (X = 9, Y = 1)

- Letter C   (X = _____, Y = _____)

- Letter E   (X = _____, Y = _____)

Lesson 57

Part 1

a.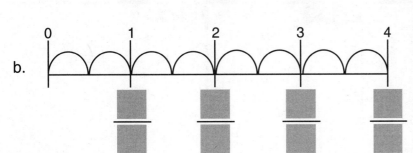

b.

Part 2

a. $\begin{array}{r} 2 \\ \times\,5 \\ \hline \end{array}$ b. $\begin{array}{r} 3 \\ \times\,5 \\ \hline \end{array}$

c. $\begin{array}{r} 5 \\ \times\,5 \\ \hline \end{array}$ d. $\begin{array}{r} 4 \\ \times\,5 \\ \hline \end{array}$

e. $\begin{array}{r} 1 \\ \times\,5 \\ \hline \end{array}$

Part 3

		Total
21		52
	19	46
Total 48	50	

Part 4

a. _____   d. _____

b. _____   e. _____

c. _____   f. _____

Part 5

a. 11 − 6 = _____   b. 11 − 7 = _____   c. 12 − 6 = _____   d. 12 − 8 = _____

e. 10 − 6 = _____   f. 10 − 5 = _____   g. 9 − 6 = _____   h. 9 − 5 = _____

i. 12 − 6 = _____   j. 11 − 6 = _____   k. 12 − 4 = _____   l. 10 − 6 = _____

m. 9 − 6 = _____   n. 11 − 6 = _____   o. 8 − 6 = _____

Do the independent work for Lesson 57 of your textbook.

Lesson 58

a. $5 \times 4 =$ _____   b. $5 \times 3 =$ _____   c. $5 \times 5 =$ _____   d. $5 \times 2 =$ _____

e. $3 \times 5 =$ _____   f. $5 \times 1 =$ _____   g. $2 \times 5 =$ _____   h. $4 \times 5 =$ _____

i. $5 \times 5 =$ _____   j. $5 \times 3 =$ _____   k. $5 \times 4 =$ _____   l. $5 \times 2 =$ _____

Part 2

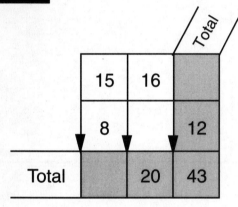

Part 3

a. _____

b. _____

c. _____

d. _____

e. _____

Part 5

a. $12 - 4 =$ _____

b. $12 - 6 =$ _____

c. $10 - 5 =$ _____

d. $10 - 6 =$ _____

e. $10 - 4 =$ _____

f. $11 - 6 =$ _____

g. $11 - 7 =$ _____

h. $12 - 8 =$ _____

i. $9 - 6 =$ _____

j. $9 - 7 =$ _____

k. $10 - 6 =$ _____

l. $10 - 8 =$ _____

m. $12 - 6 =$ _____

n. $9 - 6 =$ _____

o. $11 - 6 =$ _____

Part 4   Write the fraction for each inch.

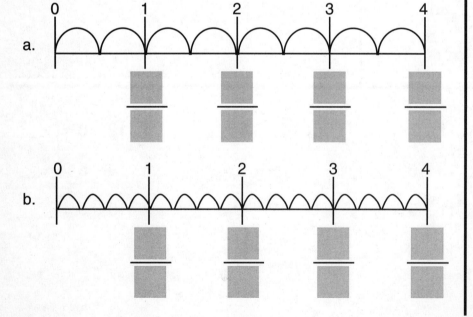

Do the independent work for Lesson 58 of your textbook.

92

Lesson 59

Part 1

a. _____

b. _____

c. _____

d. _____

e. _____

Part 2

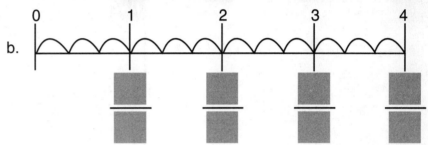

Part 3

a.	b.	c.	d.	e.	f.
5	5	5	5	3	5
x 1	x 4	x 2	x 3	x 5	x 5

g.	h.	i.	j.	k.	l.
1	5	2	3	4	5
x 5	x 4	x 5	x 5	x 5	x 5

Part 4

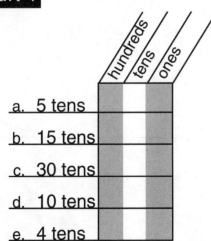

a. 5 tens

b. 15 tens

c. 30 tens

d. 10 tens

e. 4 tens

Part 5

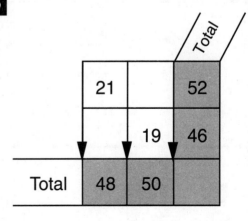

Lesson 60

Part 1

a. 5
x3

b. 10
x 4

c. 2
x5

d. 1
x7

e. 5
x5

f. 2
x6

g. 4
x5

h. 4
x3

i. 1
x5

j. 2
x4

k. 3
x4

l. 5
x4

m. 5
x5

n. 2
x7

o. 5
x1

p. 2
x9

q. 3
x5

r. 8
x2

s. 5
x2

t. 4
x4

Part 2

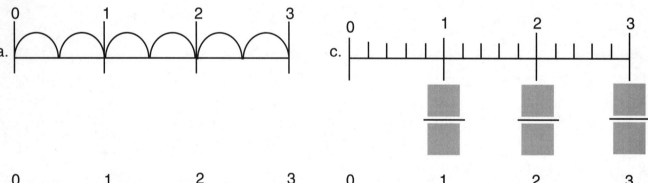

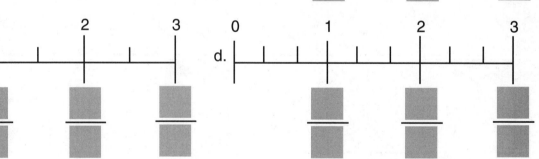

Part 3

a. 40
x 3

b. 20
x 7

c. 80
x 2

d. 30
x 5

e. 50
x 5

a. $3 \longrightarrow 9$ | d. $5 \longrightarrow 9$ | g. $4 \longrightarrow 9$ | j. $5 \longrightarrow 10$

b. $3 \longrightarrow 8$ | e. $6 \longrightarrow 12$ | h. $3 \longrightarrow 9$ | k. $4 \longrightarrow 10$

c. $5 \longrightarrow 10$ | f. $4 \longrightarrow 10$ | i. $5 \longrightarrow 11$ | l. $3 \longrightarrow 8$

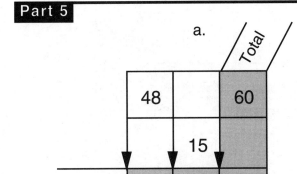

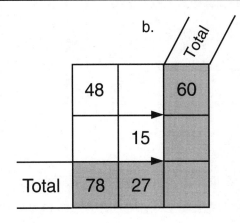

Part 5

Test 6

a. _____ | c. _____

b. _____ | d. _____

a. $7 - 6 = $ _____   c. $9 - 6 = $ _____   e. $9 - 6 = $ _____

b. $11 - 6 = $ _____   d. $12 - 6 = $ _____   f. $10 - 6 = $ _____

a. $\begin{array}{r} 5 \\ \times 1 \\ \hline \end{array}$ b. $\begin{array}{r} 3 \\ \times 5 \\ \hline \end{array}$ c. $\begin{array}{r} 2 \\ \times 5 \\ \hline \end{array}$ d. $\begin{array}{r} 5 \\ \times 4 \\ \hline \end{array}$ e. $\begin{array}{r} 5 \\ \times 5 \\ \hline \end{array}$ f. $\begin{array}{r} 5 \\ \times 2 \\ \hline \end{array}$ g. $\begin{array}{r} 4 \\ \times 5 \\ \hline \end{array}$ h. $\begin{array}{r} 5 \\ \times 3 \\ \hline \end{array}$

Part 4

Write the numerals.

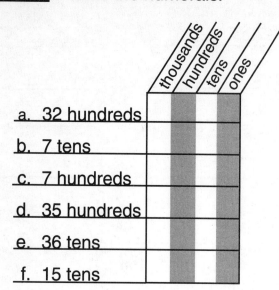

a. 32 hundreds

b. 7 tens

c. 7 hundreds

d. 35 hundreds

e. 36 tens

f. 15 tens

Part 5 Write the addition or subtraction problem and the answer for each column. Then write the missing numbers in the table.

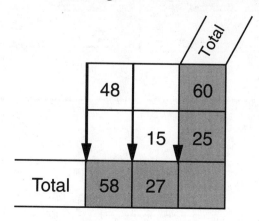

Part 6 Make a number family for each problem. Write the addition or subtraction problem and answer for each family.

a. You have □.
You find 23.
You end up with 97.

b. You have 206.
You lose 13.
You end up with □.

Part 7 Write the fractions.

a.

0   1   2   3

b.

0   1   2   3

Part 8 Write the numbers you say when you count by nines.

9 _____ _____ _____ _____ _____ _____ _____ 90

Test 6/Extra Practice

Part 1

a. _____   b. _____   c. _____   d. _____   e. _____   f. _____

Part 2

a. 11 – 6 = _____   b. 9 – 6 = _____   c. 12 – 6 = _____   d. 10 – 6 = _____

e. 12 – 6 = _____   f. 10 – 6 = _____   g. 9 – 6 = _____   h. 11 – 6 = _____

Part 3

a. 5 x 4 = _____   b. 5 x 3 = _____   c. 5 x 5 = _____   d. 5 x 2 = _____

e. 3 x 5 = _____   f. 5 x 1 = _____   g. 2 x 5 = _____   h. 4 x 5 = _____

i. 5 x 5 = _____   j. 5 x 3 = _____   k. 5 x 4 = _____   l. 5 x 2 = _____

Part 4

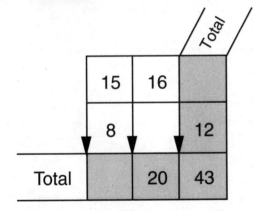

		Total
15	16	
8 ↓	↓	12 ↓
Total	20	43

Part 5 Write the fraction for each inch.

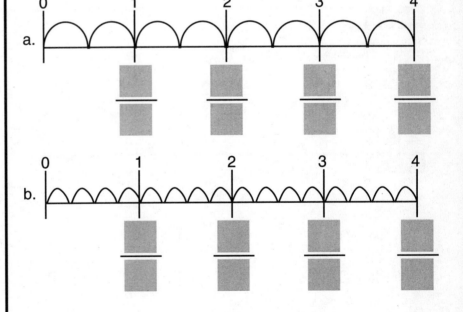

97

Lesson 61

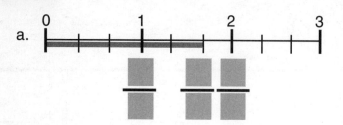

a.

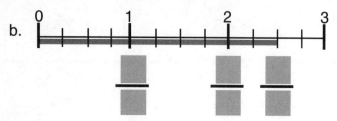

b.

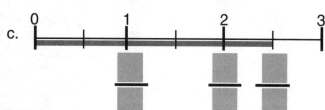

c.

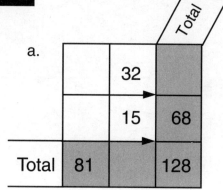

a.

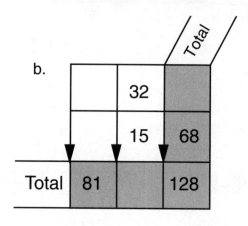

b.

Part 3

a.
$$\begin{array}{r} 300 \\ \times 4 \\ \hline 00 \end{array}$$

b.
$$\begin{array}{r} 500 \\ \times 4 \\ \hline 00 \end{array}$$

c.
$$\begin{array}{r} 900 \\ \times 2 \\ \hline \end{array}$$

d.
$$\begin{array}{r} 600 \\ \times 2 \\ \hline \end{array}$$

e.
$$\begin{array}{r} 500 \\ \times 3 \\ \hline \end{array}$$

Part 4

a. $8 - 2 =$ _____

b. $11 - 5 =$ _____

c. $10 - 5 =$ _____

d. $10 - 4 =$ _____

e. $9 - 3 =$ _____

f. $9 - 4 =$ _____

g. $11 - 5 =$ _____

h. $8 - 3 =$ _____

i. $8 - 2 =$ _____

j. $9 - 3 =$ _____

k. $8 - 3 =$ _____

l. $10 - 4 =$ _____

Lesson 62

Part 1

a.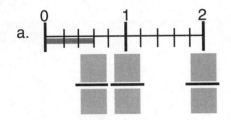
$$\begin{array}{r} 400 \\ \times\ \ 5 \\ \hline \end{array}$$

b.
$$\begin{array}{r} 500 \\ \times\ \ 5 \\ \hline \end{array}$$

c.
$$\begin{array}{r} 400 \\ \times\ \ 3 \\ \hline \end{array}$$

d.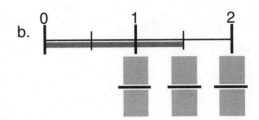
$$\begin{array}{r} 200 \\ \times\ \ 7 \\ \hline \end{array}$$

e.
$$\begin{array}{r} 200 \\ \times\ \ 8 \\ \hline \end{array}$$

Part 2

a.

b.

Part 3

a. 5___   b. 8___   c. 3___

d. 6___   e. 4___   f. 7___

g. 2___   h. 1___

Part 4

a. $10 - 5 =$ _____   h. $9 - 4 =$ _____

b. $8 - 3 =$ _____   i. $12 - 6 =$ _____

c. $11 - 5 =$ _____   j. $8 - 2 =$ _____

d. $9 - 4 =$ _____   k. $10 - 4 =$ _____

e. $10 - 4 =$ _____   l. $9 - 4 =$ _____

f. $8 - 3 =$ _____   m. $11 - 5 =$ _____

g. $9 - 3 =$ _____   n. $9 - 3 =$ _____

Part 5

a. 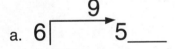 6 →⁹ 5___

b. 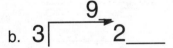 3 →⁹ 2___

c. 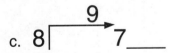 8 →⁹ 7___

d. 4 →⁹ 3___

e. 2 →⁹ 1___

f. 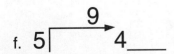 5 →⁹ 4___

Part 6

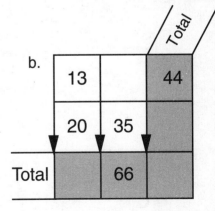

a.

		Total
13		44
20	35	
Total	66	

b.

		Total
13		44
20	35	
Total	66	

Lesson 63

Part 1

a. $7 \xrightarrow{9} 6\_\_$ b. $4 \xrightarrow{9} 3\_\_$ c. $2 \xrightarrow{9} 1\_\_$ d. $6 \xrightarrow{9} 5\_\_$

e. $3 \xrightarrow{9} 2\_\_$ f. $5 \xrightarrow{9} 4\_\_$ g. $9 \xrightarrow{9} 8\_\_$ h. $8 \xrightarrow{9} 7\_\_$

Part 2

a. $1 \xrightarrow{8} \_\_\_$ i. $1 \xrightarrow{\quad} 4$

b. $1 \xrightarrow{10} \_\_\_$ j. $1 \xrightarrow{\quad} 6$

c. $2 \xrightarrow{4} \_\_\_$ k. $1 \xrightarrow{\quad} 8$

d. $2 \xrightarrow{5} \_\_\_$ l. $1 \xrightarrow{\quad} 10$

e. $1 \xrightarrow{6} \_\_\_$ m. $2 \xrightarrow{\quad} 10$

f. $1 \xrightarrow{4} \_\_\_$ n. $2 \xrightarrow{\quad} 8$

g. $2 \xrightarrow{3} \_\_\_$ o. $2 \xrightarrow{\quad} 6$

h. $2 \xrightarrow{2} \_\_\_$ p. $2 \xrightarrow{\quad} 4$

Part 3

a.

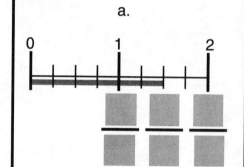

b.

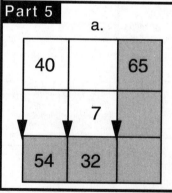

Part 4

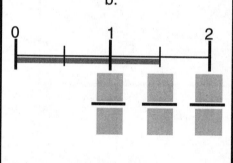

Part 5

a.

40		65
	7	
54	32	

b.

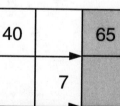

40		65
	7	
54	32	

Part 6

a. $\begin{array}{r} 600 \\ \times\ \ 2 \\ \hline \end{array}$

b. $\begin{array}{r} 50 \\ \times\ 5 \\ \hline \end{array}$

c. $\begin{array}{r} 200 \\ \times\ \ 9 \\ \hline \end{array}$

d. $\begin{array}{r} 200 \\ \times\ \ 4 \\ \hline \end{array}$

e. $\begin{array}{r} 50 \\ \times\ 3 \\ \hline \end{array}$

f. $\begin{array}{r} 40 \\ \times\ 5 \\ \hline \end{array}$

Lesson 64

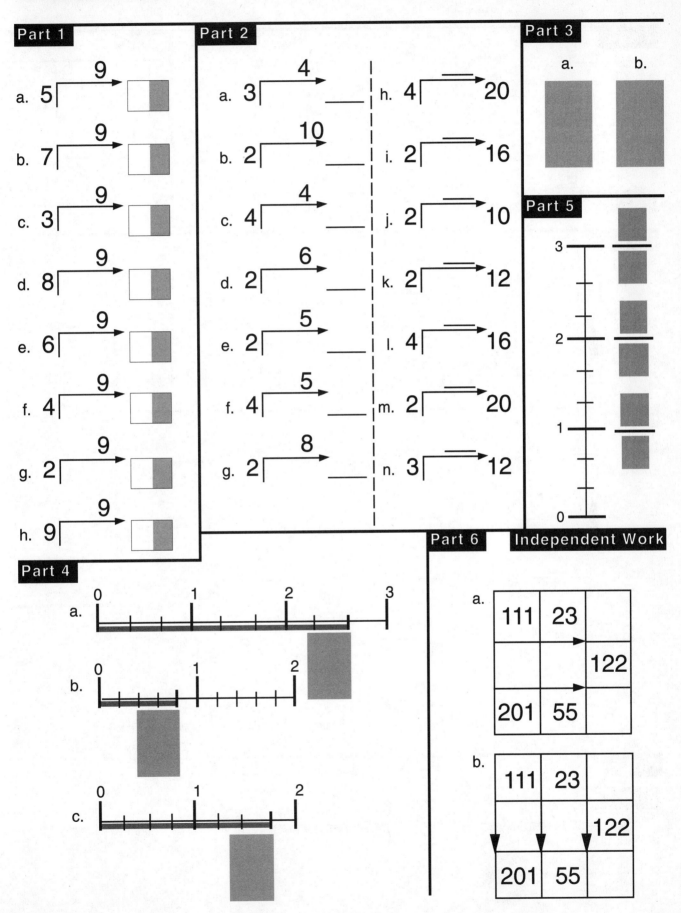

Part 1

a. 5 →9
b. 7 →9
c. 3 →9
d. 8 →9
e. 6 →9
f. 4 →9
g. 2 →9
h. 9 →9

Part 2

a. 3 →4 ___
b. 2 →10 ___
c. 4 →4 ___
d. 2 →6 ___
e. 2 →5 ___
f. 4 →5 ___
g. 2 →8 ___

h. 4 → 20
i. 2 → 16
j. 2 → 10
k. 2 → 12
l. 4 → 16
m. 2 → 20
n. 3 → 12

Part 3

a.   b.

Part 5

3
2
1
0

Part 4

a. 0 ─── 1 ─── 2 ─── 3

b. 0 ─── 1 ─── 2

c. 0 ─── 1 ─── 2

Part 6 — Independent Work

a.

111	23	
		122
201	55	

b.

111	23	
		122
201	55	

101

Lesson 65

Part 1

 a. 7 $\xrightarrow{9}$ ⬜   b. 4 $\xrightarrow{9}$ ⬜   c. 3 $\xrightarrow{9}$ ⬜

d. 2 $\xrightarrow{9}$ ⬜   e. 9 $\xrightarrow{9}$ ⬜   f. 5 $\xrightarrow{9}$ ⬜

g. 8 $\xrightarrow{9}$ ⬜   h. 6 $\xrightarrow{9}$ ⬜

Part 2

49	13	
18		
	64	131

Part 3

a. 0 — 1 — 2 — 3 $\underline{5}$

b. 0 — 1 — 2 — 3 $\underline{4}$

c. 0 — 1 — 2 — 3 $\underline{7}$

d. 0 — 1 — 2 — 3 $\underline{1}$

Part 4

a. 2 $\xrightarrow{\quad}$ 10   f. 4 $\xrightarrow{\quad}$ 40   k. 7 $\xrightarrow{\quad}$ 70

b. 1 $\xrightarrow{\quad}$ 7   g. 7 $\xrightarrow{\quad}$ 70   l. 1 $\xrightarrow{\quad}$ 3

c. 4 $\xrightarrow{\quad}$ 20   h. 1 $\xrightarrow{\quad}$ 5   m. 1 $\xrightarrow{\quad}$ 8

d. 3 $\xrightarrow{\quad}$ 30   i. 8 $\xrightarrow{\quad}$ 80   n. 9 $\xrightarrow{\quad}$ 90

e. 5 $\xrightarrow{\quad}$ 50   j. 1 $\xrightarrow{\quad}$ 9   o. 1 $\xrightarrow{\quad}$ 6

Part 5

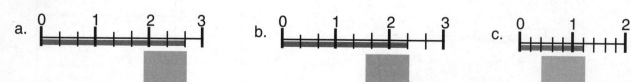

a. 0 — 1 — 2 — 3   b. 0 — 1 — 2 — 3   c. 0 — 1 — 2

Lesson 66

a. 0 1 2 [4]

b. 0 1 2 [3]

c. 0 1 2 [3]

Part 2

a. 6 x 9 = ____   b. 2 x 9 = ____   c. 4 x 9 = ____   d. 8 x 9 = ____

e. 9 x 9 = ____   f. 7 x 9 = ____   g. 3 x 9 = ____   h. 5 x 9 = ____

Part 3

a. $\begin{array}{r} 50 \\ \times\ 6 \\ \hline \end{array}$ b. $\begin{array}{r} 300 \\ \times\ 2 \\ \hline \end{array}$ c. $\begin{array}{r} 300 \\ \times\ 5 \\ \hline \end{array}$ d. $\begin{array}{r} 800 \\ \times\ 2 \\ \hline \end{array}$ e. $\begin{array}{r} 80 \\ \times\ 5 \\ \hline \end{array}$

Part 4

a.   b.   c.

 0 1 2 3 [—]

 0 1 2 3 [—]

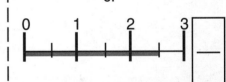 0 1 2 3 [—]

Part 5

a. 1 ⌐→ 4   g. 2 ⌐→ 6   m. 2 ⌐→ 10

b. 2 ⌐→ 4   h. 7 ⌐→ 70   n. 2 ⌐→ 4

c. 2 ⌐→ 6   i. 2 ⌐→ 10   o. 2 ⌐→ 6

d. 2 ⌐→ 8   j. 1 ⌐→ 6   p. 2 ⌐→ 8

e. 2 ⌐→ 10   k. 2 ⌐→ 4

f. 5 ⌐→ 50   l. 2 ⌐→ 8

Lesson 67

Part 1

a. [number line 0 to 2] $\underline{5}$

b. [number line 0 to 2] $\underline{3}$

c. [number line 0 to 2] $\underline{3}$

Part 2

a. $2\,\overline{}\!\!\rightarrow 8$

b. $2\,\overline{}\!\!\rightarrow 10$

c. $2\,\overline{}\!\!\rightarrow 12$

d. $2\,\overline{}\!\!\rightarrow 4$

e. $2\,\overline{}\!\!\rightarrow 20$

f. $2\,\overline{}\!\!\rightarrow 18$

g. $1\,\overline{}\!\!\rightarrow 9$

h. $7\,\overline{}\!\!\rightarrow 70$

i. $2\,\overline{}\!\!\rightarrow 12$

j. $2\,\overline{}\!\!\rightarrow 8$

k. $1\,\overline{}\!\!\rightarrow 10$

l. $6\,\overline{}\!\!\rightarrow 60$

Part 3

a. [number line 0 to 2]

b. [number line 0 to 2]

c. [number line 0 to 2]

d. [number line 0 to 2]

Part 4

a.
$$\begin{array}{r} 20 \\ \times\ 8 \\ \hline \end{array}$$

b.
$$\begin{array}{r} 600 \\ \times\ \ 5 \\ \hline \end{array}$$

c.
$$\begin{array}{r} 600 \\ \times\ \ 2 \\ \hline \end{array}$$

d.
$$\begin{array}{r} 20 \\ \times\ 7 \\ \hline \end{array}$$

e.
$$\begin{array}{r} 900 \\ \times\ \ 5 \\ \hline \end{array}$$

Part 5 — Independent Work

a. 5 x 9 = _____

b. 7 x 9 = _____

c. 9 x 9 = _____

d. 3 x 9 = _____

e. 8 x 9 = _____

f. 6 x 9 = _____

g. 4 x 9 = _____

h. 2 x 9 = _____

Lesson 68

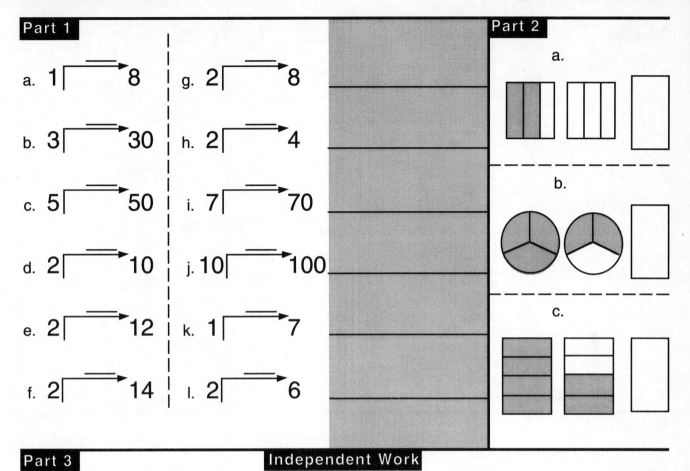

a. 1⟌8 g. 2⟌8

b. 3⟌30 h. 2⟌4

c. 5⟌50 i. 7⟌70

d. 2⟌10 j. 10⟌100

e. 2⟌12 k. 1⟌7

f. 2⟌14 l. 2⟌6

Part 2

a.

b.

c.

Part 3   Independent Work

Write the bottom number for each fraction. Then shade the number of parts.

a. 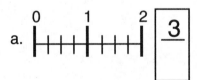 0 1 2 [3]

b. 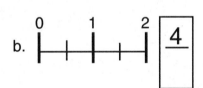 0 1 2 [4]

c.  0 1 2 [6]

Lesson 69

Part 1

a. 6 ⟶ 60
b. 1 ⟶ 4
c. 5 ⟶ 50
d. 1 ⟶ 10
e. 2 ⟶ 10
f. 2 ⟶ 12

g. 2 ⟶ 16
h. 2 ⟶ 20
i. 2 ⟶ 18
j. 2 ⟶ 14
k. 2 ⟶ 6
l. 2 ⟶ 8

Part 2

	Monday	Tuesday	Total for both days
Red birds	21		99
Yellow birds	54	31	
Total birds			184

a. How many yellow birds were seen on Tuesday? _____

b. How many total birds were seen on Monday? _____

c. How many red birds were seen on Monday? _____

d. How many total birds were seen on Tuesday? _____

Part 3 — Independent Work

Write the bottom number for each fraction. Then shade the number of parts.

a. 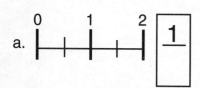 1

b. 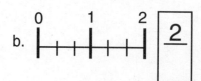 2

c.  8

106

Lesson 70

Part 1

a. 4 ⌐ 4 → ___
b. 4 ⌐ 5 → ___
c. 4 ⌐ 6 → ___
d. 4 ⌐ 7 → ___
e. 4 ⌐ 8 → ___
f. 4 ⌐ 9 → ___
g. 4 ⌐ 10 → ___

h. 4 ⌐ 5 → ___
i. 4 ⌐ 6 → ___
j. 4 ⌐ 8 → ___
k. 4 ⌐ 9 → ___
l. 4 ⌐ 7 → ___
m. 4 ⌐ 4 → ___
n. 4 ⌐ 10 → ___

Part 2

	Sunday	Monday	Total for both days
Big clouds	35	17	
Small clouds			91
Total clouds	51		143

a. How many big clouds and small clouds were seen on both days?

_____

b. Were there more big clouds or more small clouds seen on Monday?

_____

c. How many total clouds were seen on Monday?

_____

d. Were there more total clouds on Sunday or Monday?

_____

Part 3

a. 2 ⌐ ___ → 20
b. 2 ⌐ ___ → 10
c. 2 ⌐ ___ → 12
d. 2 ⌐ ___ → 14
e. 2 ⌐ ___ → 18
f. 2 ⌐ ___ → 16

g. 5 ⌐ ___ → 50
h. 2 ⌐ ___ → 6
i. 1 ⌐ ___ → 5
j. 5 ⌐ ___ → 25
k. 2 ⌐ ___ → 8
l. 2 ⌐ ___ → 14

Test 7

Part 1

a. 2⟶8 f. 2⟶18

b. 2⟶10 g. 1⟶9

c. 2⟶12 h. 7⟶70

d. 2⟶4 i. 1⟶10

e. 2⟶20 j. 6⟶60

Part 2

a. 10 − 5 = ____ g. 10 − 1 = ____

b. 12 − 6 = ____ h. 9 − 4 = ____

c. 11 − 5 = ____ i. 8 − 2 = ____

d. 9 − 3 = ____ j. 8 − 1 = ____

e. 10 − 4 = ____ k. 8 − 3 = ____

f. 8 − 3 = ____ l. 7 − 1 = ____

Part 3 Write the fractions.

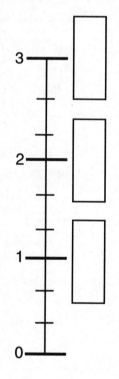

Part 4 Fill in all the missing numbers.

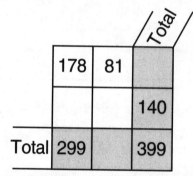

		Total
178	81	
		140
Total 299		399

Part 5 For each problem, complete the fraction and shade the line.

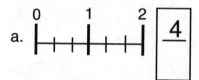

a. 0 1 2 $\dfrac{}{4}$

b. 0 1 2 $\dfrac{}{3}$

108

a.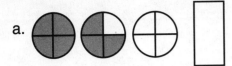

b.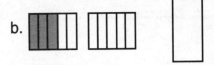

Go to Test 7 in your textbook.

Start

$$\xrightarrow[2]{1 \quad 1} \xrightarrow[3]{1 \quad 2} \xrightarrow[4]{1 \quad 3} \xrightarrow[5]{1 \quad 4} \xrightarrow[6]{1 \quad 5} \xrightarrow[7]{1 \quad 6} \xrightarrow[8]{1 \quad 7} \xrightarrow[9]{1 \quad 8} \xrightarrow[10]{1 \quad 9} \xrightarrow[11]{1 \quad 10}$$

$$\xrightarrow[4]{2 \quad 2} \xrightarrow[5]{2 \quad 3} \xrightarrow[6]{2 \quad 4} \xrightarrow[7]{2 \quad 5} \xrightarrow[8]{2 \quad 6} \xrightarrow[9]{2 \quad 7} \xrightarrow[10]{2 \quad 8} \xrightarrow[11]{2 \quad 9} \xrightarrow[12]{2 \quad 10}$$

$$\xrightarrow[6]{3 \quad 3} \xrightarrow[7]{3 \quad 4} \xrightarrow[8]{3 \quad 5} \xrightarrow[9]{3 \quad 6} \xrightarrow[10]{3 \quad 7} \xrightarrow[11]{3 \quad 8} \xrightarrow[12]{3 \quad 9} \xrightarrow[13]{3 \quad 10}$$

$$\xrightarrow[8]{4 \quad 4} \xrightarrow[9]{4 \quad 5} \xrightarrow[10]{4 \quad 6} \xrightarrow[11]{4 \quad 7} \xrightarrow[12]{4 \quad 8} \xrightarrow[13]{4 \quad 9} \xrightarrow[14]{4 \quad 10}$$

$$\xrightarrow[10]{5 \quad 5}$$ $$\xrightarrow[14]{5 \quad 9} \xrightarrow[15]{5 \quad 10}$$

$$\xrightarrow[15]{6 \quad 9} \xrightarrow[16]{6 \quad 10}$$

Test Lesson 7

$$\xrightarrow[16]{7 \quad 9} \xrightarrow[17]{7 \quad 10}$$

$$\xrightarrow[17]{8 \quad 9} \xrightarrow[18]{8 \quad 10}$$

Fact Game

$$\xrightarrow[18]{9 \quad 9} \xrightarrow[19]{9 \quad 10}$$

Finish $$\xrightarrow[20]{10 \quad 10}$$

Test 7/Extra Practice

Part 1

a. $1\overline{)4}$ g. $2\overline{)6}$ m. $2\overline{)10}$

b. $2\overline{)4}$ h. $7\overline{)70}$ n. $2\overline{)4}$

c. $2\overline{)6}$ i. $2\overline{)10}$ o. $2\overline{)6}$

d. $2\overline{)8}$ j. $1\overline{)6}$ p. $2\overline{)8}$

e. $2\overline{)10}$ k. $2\overline{)4}$

f. $5\overline{)50}$ l. $2\overline{)8}$

Part 2

a. $10 - 5 = \underline{\hspace{1cm}}$ h. $9 - 4 = \underline{\hspace{1cm}}$

b. $8 - 3 = \underline{\hspace{1cm}}$ i. $12 - 6 = \underline{\hspace{1cm}}$

c. $11 - 5 = \underline{\hspace{1cm}}$ j. $8 - 2 = \underline{\hspace{1cm}}$

d. $9 - 4 = \underline{\hspace{1cm}}$ k. $10 - 4 = \underline{\hspace{1cm}}$

e. $10 - 4 = \underline{\hspace{1cm}}$ l. $9 - 4 = \underline{\hspace{1cm}}$

f. $8 - 3 = \underline{\hspace{1cm}}$ m. $11 - 5 = \underline{\hspace{1cm}}$

g. $9 - 3 = \underline{\hspace{1cm}}$ n. $9 - 3 = \underline{\hspace{1cm}}$

Part 3

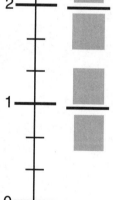

Part 4

a. 0 1 2 3 $\boxed{\underline{5}}$

b. 0 1 2 3 $\boxed{\underline{4}}$

c. 0 1 2 3 $\boxed{\underline{7}}$

d. 0 1 2 3 $\boxed{\underline{1}}$

Lesson 71

Part 1

a. $4 \overline{\smash{\big)}}^{\,7} \longrightarrow$ _____

b. $4 \overline{\smash{\big)}}^{\,5} \longrightarrow$ _____

c. $4 \overline{\smash{\big)}}^{\,8} \longrightarrow$ _____

d. $4 \overline{\smash{\big)}}^{\,6} \longrightarrow$ _____

Part 2

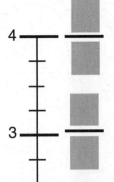

Part 3

a. $7 \overline{\smash{\big)}} \longrightarrow 70$

b. $2 \overline{\smash{\big)}} \longrightarrow 20$

c. $2 \overline{\smash{\big)}} \longrightarrow 16$

d. $2 \overline{\smash{\big)}} \longrightarrow 12$

e. $2 \overline{\smash{\big)}} \longrightarrow 18$

f. $3 \overline{\smash{\big)}} \longrightarrow 30$

g. $1 \overline{\smash{\big)}} \longrightarrow 7$

h. $2 \overline{\smash{\big)}} \longrightarrow 10$

i. $5 \overline{\smash{\big)}} \longrightarrow 25$

j. $2 \overline{\smash{\big)}} \longrightarrow 6$

Part 4

a. $10 - \underline{\hphantom{00}} = \underline{\hphantom{00}}$

b. $16 - \underline{\hphantom{00}} = \underline{\hphantom{00}}$

c. $6 - \underline{\hphantom{00}} = \underline{\hphantom{00}}$

d. $8 - \underline{\hphantom{00}} = \underline{\hphantom{00}}$

e. $14 - \underline{\hphantom{00}} = \underline{\hphantom{00}}$

f. $12 - \underline{\hphantom{00}} = \underline{\hphantom{00}}$

g. $4 - \underline{\hphantom{00}} = \underline{\hphantom{00}}$

h. $16 - \underline{\hphantom{00}} = \underline{\hphantom{00}}$

i. $18 - \underline{\hphantom{00}} = \underline{\hphantom{00}}$

j. $14 - \underline{\hphantom{00}} = \underline{\hphantom{00}}$

Part 5   Independent Work

472		565
137		
		961

Lesson 72

Part 1

a. 1⟌ 9   f. 2⟌ 18 _____

b. 2⟌ 8   g. 4⟌ 40 _____

c. 2⟌ 4   h. 1⟌ 3 _____

d. 2⟌ 12   i. 2⟌ 16 _____

e. 9⟌ 90   j. 2⟌ 14 _____

Part 2   Independent Work

Write the bottom number for each fraction. Then shade the parts.

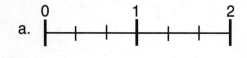
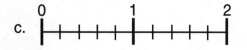

a. 0 ——1——2 | 5 |

b. 0 ——1——2 | 1 |

c. 0 ——1——2 | 4 |

d. 0 ——1——2 | 3 |

Part 3   Write each letter where it belongs on the grid.

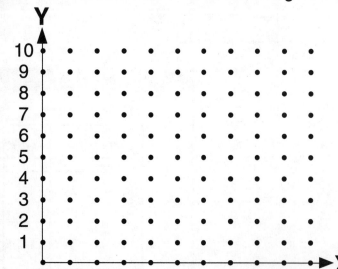

Letter A. (X = 0, Y = 4)

Letter B. (X = 7, Y = 5)

Letter C. (X = 4, Y = 3)

Letter D. (X = 8, Y = 10)

112

Lesson 73

a. $10 - 3 =$ _____   b. $11 - 3 =$ _____   c. $6 - 3 =$ _____   d. $9 - 3 =$ _____

e. $13 - 3 =$ _____   f. $11 - 3 =$ _____   g. $10 - 3 =$ _____   h. $12 - 3 =$ _____

i. $8 - 3 =$ _____

Part 2

a. $\frac{5}{3}$ more than 1 unit
   less than 1 unit

b. $\frac{7}{4}$ more than 1 unit
   less than 1 unit

c. $\frac{1}{2}$ more than 1 unit
   less than 1 unit

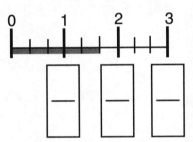

d. $\frac{7}{5}$ more than 1 unit
   less than 1 unit

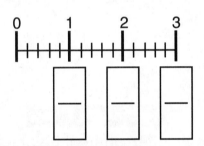

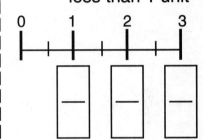

Part 3

a. $2\overline{\smash{)}20}$

b. $1\overline{\smash{)}10}$

c. $2\overline{\smash{)}16}$

d. $1\overline{\smash{)}8}$

e. $7\overline{\smash{)}70}$

f. $2\overline{\smash{)}14}$

g. $2\overline{\smash{)}18}$

h. $2\overline{\smash{)}12}$

i. $2\overline{\smash{)}20}$

j. $2\overline{\smash{)}16}$

Do the independent work for Lesson 73 of your textbook.

Lesson 74

Part 1

a. 4 x 7 = ____ b. 4 x 9 = ____ c. 4 x 8 = ____ d. 4 x 6 = ____

e. 5 x 4 = ____ f. 7 x 4 = ____ g. 10 x 4 = ____ h. 8 x 4 = ____

i. 4 x 6 = ____ j. 8 x 4 = ____ k. 4 x 5 = ____ l. 4 x 9 = ____

Part 2

a. 5⟌25   f. 2⟌20 _____

b. 2⟌12   g. 2⟌18 _____

c. 1⟌6   h. 2⟌14 _____

d. 8⟌80   i. 2⟌16 _____

e. 2⟌18   j. 2⟌12 _____

Part 3

Circle **more than 1 unit** or **less than 1 unit.** Then shade the parts.

a. $\frac{1}{2}$ more than 1 unit
         less than 1 unit

b. $\frac{5}{3}$ more than 1 unit
         less than 1 unit

c. $\frac{4}{2}$ more than 1 unit
         less than 1 unit

d. $\frac{3}{4}$ more than 1 unit
         less than 1 unit

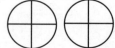

Part 4   Independent Work

Write each letter where it belongs on the grid.

A. (X = 1, Y = 8)   C. (X = 4, Y = 5)

B. (X = 6, Y = 3)   D. (X = 10, Y = 0)

Lesson 75

a. _____ b. _____ c. _____ d. _____ e. _____

Part 2 Circle **more than 1, less than 1** or **equal to 1.** Then shade the parts in the picture.

a. $\frac{4}{4}$ more than 1
less than 1
equal to 1

b. $\frac{2}{2}$ more than 1
less than 1
equal to 1

c. $\frac{6}{5}$ more than 1
less than 1
equal to 1

d. $\frac{4}{5}$ more than 1
less than 1
equal to 1

e. $\frac{5}{5}$ more than 1
less than 1
equal to 1

Part 3

a.   9 x 4 = _____   f. 7 x 4 = _____

b. 10 x 4 = _____   g. 4 x 4 = _____

c.   6 x 4 = _____   h. 4 x 8 = _____

d.   5 x 4 = _____   i. 4 x 6 = _____

e.   8 x 4 = _____   j. 4 x 9 = _____

Part 4   Write the missing numbers.

a. 2⌐‾→16   e. 2⌐‾→10

b. 1⌐‾→7   f. 2⌐‾→8

c. 5⌐‾→20   g. 2⌐‾→4

d. 3⌐‾→30   h. 10⌐‾→70

Part 5   **Independent Work**
Figure out the answers.

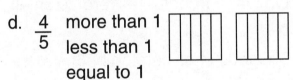

a.   50
    x 7

b. 600
    x   9

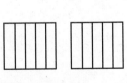

c. 800
    x   1

d.   3
    x 4

Part 6   Complete the subtraction facts. Each fact has small numbers that are the same.

a. 10 – _____ = _____   d. 8 – _____ = _____

b. 16 – _____ = _____   e. 14 – _____ = _____

c. 6 – _____ = _____   f. 12 – _____ = _____

115

Lesson 76

Part 1

a. 10 – 3 = _____   10 – 7 = _____

b. 11 – 3 = _____   11 – 8 = _____

c. 13 – 3 = _____   13 – 10 = _____

d. 9 – 3 = _____   9 – 6 = _____

Part 2

a. 14 – 7 = _____   f. 10 – 7 = _____

b. 16 – 8 = _____   g. 4 – 2 = _____

c. 11 – 8 = _____   h. 11 – 8 = _____

d. 12 – 6 = _____   i. 6 – 3 = _____

e. 10 – 5 = _____   i. 10 – 7 = _____

Part 3

The table is supposed to show the cars that were on two different streets.

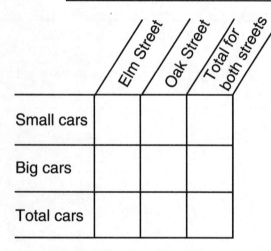

	Elm Street	Oak Street	Total for both streets
Small cars			
Big cars			
Total cars			

Fact 1: On Elm Street there were 76 cars in all.

Fact 2: The total of all small cars was 49.

Fact 3: On Oak Street there were 20 small cars.

Fact 4: The total of all cars on both streets was 140.

a. Were there more big cars on Elm Street or Oak Street? _____

b. How many big cars were on Oak Street? _____

c. How many total big cars were there? _____

d. Were there more big cars or small cars? _____

e. Were there more cars on Elm Street or on Oak Street? _____

Part 4

a. 2 x _____ = 8   b. 2 x _____ = 18   c. 1 x _____ = 5   d. 2 x _____ = 14

e. 5 x _____ = 25   f. 2 x _____ = 10   g. 9 x _____ = 90   h. 2 x _____ = 16

i. 2 x _____ = 12   j. 2 x _____ = 20

a. $\frac{8}{6}$ more than 1
      less than 1
      equal to 1

b. $\frac{6}{8}$ more than 1
      less than 1
      equal to 1

c. $\frac{6}{6}$ more than 1
      less than 1
      equal to 1

d. $\frac{8}{8}$ more than 1
      less than 1
      equal to 1

e. $\frac{7}{6}$ more than 1
      less than 1
      equal to 1

f. $\frac{5}{6}$ more than 1
      less than 1
      equal to 1

g. $\frac{9}{7}$ more than 1
      less than 1
      equal to 1

h. $\frac{7}{7}$ more than 1
      less than 1
      equal to 1

Lesson 77

Part 1

> The table is supposed to show the number of rocks in different parks.

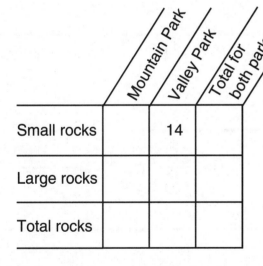

	Mountain Park	Valley Park	Total for both parks
Small rocks		14	
Large rocks			
Total rocks			

Fact 1: In Mountain Park, there are 18 rocks in all.

Fact 2: In Mountain Park, there are 10 small rocks.

Fact 3: The total number of rocks in both parks is 37.

Fact 4: In Valley Park, there are 5 large rocks.

a. Were there more large rocks in Mountain Park or Valley Park?

_____

b. How many large rocks were there in both parks? _____

c. Were there more large rocks or small rocks? _____

d. Were there more rocks in Mountain Park or Valley Park? _____

a. $\begin{array}{r} 9 \\ \times 3 \\ \hline \end{array}$ b. $\begin{array}{r} 9 \\ \times 5 \\ \hline \end{array}$ c. $\begin{array}{r} 3 \\ \times 9 \\ \hline \end{array}$ d. $\begin{array}{r} 9 \\ \times 4 \\ \hline \end{array}$ e. $\begin{array}{r} 2 \\ \times 9 \\ \hline \end{array}$ f. $\begin{array}{r} 4 \\ \times 9 \\ \hline \end{array}$ g. $\begin{array}{r} 9 \\ \times 6 \\ \hline \end{array}$ h. $\begin{array}{r} 5 \\ \times 9 \\ \hline \end{array}$

Part 3

a. $1 = \dfrac{\boxed{}}{3}$ b. $1 = \dfrac{\boxed{}}{6}$ c. $1 = \dfrac{\boxed{}}{4}$ d. $1 = \dfrac{\boxed{}}{7}$

Part 4

a. $1 = \dfrac{\boxed{}}{5}$ b. $1 \underline{} \boxed{\dfrac{6}{5}}$ c. $1 \underline{} \boxed{\dfrac{4}{5}}$ d. $1 \underline{} \boxed{\dfrac{10}{5}}$

Part 5

a. $1 = \dfrac{\boxed{}}{7}$ b. $1 \underline{} \boxed{\dfrac{5}{7}}$ c. $1 \underline{} \boxed{\dfrac{1}{7}}$ d. $1 \underline{} \boxed{\dfrac{8}{7}}$

Do the independent work for Lesson 77 of your textbook.

Lesson 78

Part 1

a. $1 = \boxed{\dfrac{}{2}}$ b. $1 \underline{} \dfrac{3}{2}$ c. $1 \underline{} \dfrac{1}{2}$ d. $1 \underline{} \dfrac{5}{2}$

Part 2

a. $1 = \boxed{\dfrac{}{10}}$ b. $1 \underline{} \dfrac{9}{10}$ c. $1 \underline{} \dfrac{20}{10}$ d. $1 \underline{} \dfrac{1}{10}$

Part 3

a. $2\overline{\smash{\big)}\,\overset{\boxed{}}{}}\!\!\rightarrow 10$ $\boxed{}\overline{\smash{\big)}\,\overset{\boxed{}}{}}\!\!\rightarrow 10$ 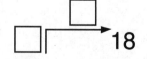 b. $2\overline{\smash{\big)}\,\overset{\boxed{}}{}}\!\!\rightarrow 18$ $\boxed{}\overline{\smash{\big)}\,\overset{\boxed{}}{}}\!\!\rightarrow 18$

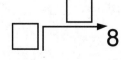 c. $2\overline{\smash{\big)}\,\overset{\boxed{}}{}}\!\!\rightarrow 8$ $\boxed{}\overline{\smash{\big)}\,\overset{\boxed{}}{}}\!\!\rightarrow 8$ 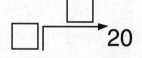 d. $2\overline{\smash{\big)}\,\overset{\boxed{}}{}}\!\!\rightarrow 20$ $\boxed{}\overline{\smash{\big)}\,\overset{\boxed{}}{}}\!\!\rightarrow 20$

The table is supposed to show the number of small and big boats that were on two different lakes.

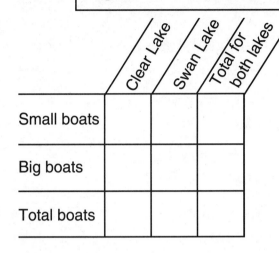

	Clear Lake	Swan Lake	Total for both lakes
Small boats			
Big boats			
Total boats			

Fact 1: There were 90 big boats on both lakes.

Fact 2: There were 31 small boats on Clear Lake.

Fact 3: There were 65 big boats on Clear Lake.

Fact 4: There were 18 small boats on Swan Lake.

a. How many small boats were on both lakes? _____

b. How many big boats were on Swan Lake? _____

c. Were there more big boats or small boats on Swan Lake? _____

Part 5

a. 9 x 7 = _____   b. 6 x 9 = _____   c. 5 x 9 = _____   d. 9 x 8 = _____

e. 9 x 6 = _____   f. 8 x 9 = _____   g. 9 x 10 = _____   h. 7 x 9 = _____

Do the independent work for Lesson 78 of your textbook.

Lesson 79

Part 1

a. 9 x 2 = _____   b. 4 x 9 = _____   c. 9 x 6 = _____   d. 9 x 5 = _____

e. 9 x 3 = _____   f. 5 x 9 = _____   g. 3 x 9 = _____   h. 9 x 4 = _____

i. 2 x 9 = _____   j. 6 x 9 = _____

The table is supposed to show the number of ducks and geese seen on two different lakes.

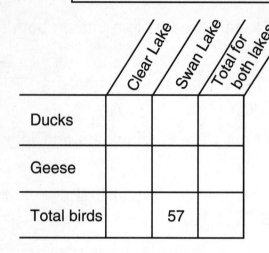

	Clear Lake	Swan Lake	Total for both lakes
Ducks			
Geese			
Total birds		57	

Fact 1: The total geese seen on both lakes was 56.

Fact 2: 20 ducks were seen on Swan Lake.

Fact 3: 19 geese were seen on Clear Lake.

Fact 4: The total birds seen on Clear Lake was 168.

a. Were there more ducks seen on Clear Lake or on Swan Lake?

_____

b. How many total ducks were seen on both lakes? _____

c. How many total birds were seen on both lakes? _____

Part 3

a. 3 ⌐ 5 → ___   ⌐ →

b. 2 ⌐ → 18   ⌐ →

c. 4 ⌐ 5 → ___   ⌐ →

d. 2 ⌐ → 14   ⌐ →

e. 2 ⌐ → 10   ⌐ →

Part 4

a. $\dfrac{\boxed{}}{4} = 1$ $\dfrac{1}{4} - 1$ $1 - \dfrac{3}{4}$ $1 - \dfrac{7}{4}$

b. $1 = \dfrac{\boxed{}}{5}$ $1 - \dfrac{4}{5}$ $1 - \dfrac{6}{5}$ $1 - \dfrac{5}{5}$

Lesson 80

Part 1

a. $9 \times 6 =$ _____   b. $5 \times 9 =$ _____   c. $9 \times 9 =$ _____   d. $9 \times 7 =$ _____

e. $6 \times 9 =$ _____   f. $9 \times 3 =$ _____   g. $9 \times 8 =$ _____   h. $10 \times 9 =$ _____

i. $9 \times 5 =$ _____   j. $7 \times 9 =$ _____   k. $8 \times 9 =$ _____   l. $9 \times 4 =$ _____

Part 2

a. $1 \underline{} \dfrac{4}{5}$ b. $1 \underline{} \dfrac{6}{4}$ c. $\dfrac{9}{8} \underline{} 1$ d. $\dfrac{7}{7} \underline{} 1$ e. $\dfrac{5}{8} \underline{} 1$

Part 3

a. $2\overline{)}\;10$

b. $3\overline{)}\;12$

c. $4\overline{)}\;16$

d. $3\overline{)}\;15$

e. $2\overline{)}\;12$

Part 4

a. $\dfrac{6+3}{4}$ $\cdots$ ☐   b. $\dfrac{6-5}{7}$ ☐   c. $\dfrac{9-4}{3}$ ☐

d. $\dfrac{10-8}{5}$ ☐   e. $\dfrac{5+6}{10}$ ☐   f. $\dfrac{12-9}{2}$ ☐

g. $\dfrac{9+9}{7}$ ☐

Test 8

a. $16 - \_\_\_ = \_\_\_$ b. $6 - \_\_\_ = \_\_\_$ c. $12 - \_\_\_ = \_\_\_$ d. $4 - \_\_\_ = \_\_\_$

e. $10 - \_\_\_ = \_\_\_$ f. $18 - \_\_\_ = \_\_\_$ g. $14 - \_\_\_ = \_\_\_$ h. $2 - \_\_\_ = \_\_\_$

Part 2

a. $3 \times 4 = \_\_\_$ b. $8 \times 4 = \_\_\_$ c. $4 \times 9 = \_\_\_$ d. $4 \times 10 = \_\_\_$

e. $5 \times 4 = \_\_\_$ f. $6 \times 4 = \_\_\_$ g. $4 \times 6 = \_\_\_$ h. $4 \times 7 = \_\_\_$

i. $7 \times 4 = \_\_\_$ j. $4 \times 4 = \_\_\_$ k. $4 \times 8 = \_\_\_$ l. $4 \times 2 = \_\_\_$

m. $9 \times 4 = \_\_\_$ n. $10 \times 4 = \_\_\_$ o. $4 \times 3 = \_\_\_$ p. $4 \times 5 = \_\_\_$

Part 3

a. $2 \times \_\_\_ = 8$ b. $2 \times \_\_\_ = 14$ c. $9 \times \_\_\_ = 90$ d. $2 \times \_\_\_ = 12$

e. $2 \times \_\_\_ = 18$ f. $5 \times \_\_\_ = 25$ g. $2 \times \_\_\_ = 16$ h. $2 \times \_\_\_ = 20$

i. $1 \times \_\_\_ = 5$ j. $2 \times \_\_\_ = 10$

Part 4

a. $\begin{array}{r} 8 \\ -3 \\ \hline \end{array}$ b. $\begin{array}{r} 10 \\ -7 \\ \hline \end{array}$ c. $\begin{array}{r} 11 \\ -8 \\ \hline \end{array}$ d. $\begin{array}{r} 11 \\ -3 \\ \hline \end{array}$ e. $\begin{array}{r} 12 \\ -8 \\ \hline \end{array}$

f. $\begin{array}{r} 6 \\ -3 \\ \hline \end{array}$ g. $\begin{array}{r} 10 \\ -3 \\ \hline \end{array}$ h. $\begin{array}{r} 13 \\ -3 \\ \hline \end{array}$ i. $\begin{array}{r} 11 \\ -7 \\ \hline \end{array}$ j. $\begin{array}{r} 7 \\ -3 \\ \hline \end{array}$

Part 5 Complete the sign. $<, =, >$

a. $\dfrac{1}{4} \_\_ 1$ b. $\dfrac{3}{4} \_\_ 1$ c. $\dfrac{7}{7} \_\_ 1$

Part 6

Complete the table. Then answer the questions.

The table is supposed to show the number of rocks in two different parks.

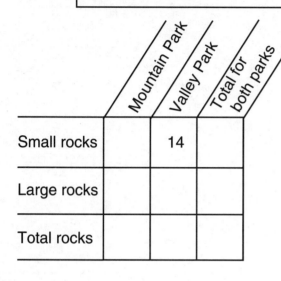

	Mountain Park	Valley Park	Total for both parks
Small rocks		14	
Large rocks			
Total rocks			

Fact 1: In Mountain Park, there are 18 total rocks.

Fact 2: In Mountain Park, there are 10 small rocks.

Fact 3: The total number of rocks in both parks is 37.

Fact 4: In Valley Park, there are 5 large rocks.

a. Were there more large rocks in Mountain Park or Valley Park?

_____

b. How many large rocks were there in both parks? _____

c. Were there more large rocks or small rocks? _____

d. Were there more rocks in Mountain Park or Valley Park?

_____

Start

$1\overline{)1}\ 1\quad 1\overline{)2}\ 2\quad 1\overline{)3}\ 3\quad 1\overline{)4}\ 4\quad 1\overline{)5}\ 5\quad 1\overline{)6}\ 6\quad 1\overline{)7}\ 7\quad 1\overline{)8}\ 8\quad 1\overline{)9}\ 9\quad 1\overline{)10}\ 10$

$2\overline{)2}\ 4\quad 2\overline{)3}\ 6\quad 2\overline{)4}\ 8\quad 2\overline{)5}\ 10\quad 2\overline{)6}\ 12\quad 2\overline{)7}\ 14\quad 2\overline{)8}\ 16\quad 2\overline{)9}\ 18\quad 2\overline{)10}\ 20$

$3\overline{)4}\ 12\quad 3\overline{)5}\ 15\qquad\qquad 3\overline{)9}\ 27\quad 3\overline{)10}\ 30$

$4\overline{)4}\ 16\quad 4\overline{)5}\ 20\qquad\qquad 4\overline{)9}\ 36\quad 4\overline{)10}\ 40$

$5\overline{)5}\ 25\qquad\qquad 5\overline{)9}\ 45\quad 5\overline{)10}\ 50$

$6\overline{)9}\ 54\quad 6\overline{)10}\ 60$

$7\overline{)9}\ 63\quad 7\overline{)10}\ 70$

$8\overline{)9}\ 72\quad 8\overline{)10}\ 80$

$9\overline{)9}\ 81\quad 9\overline{)10}\ 90$

Finish $10\overline{)10}\ 100$

Test Lesson 8

Fact Game 1

Start

$\dfrac{1}{\to}\,1_2\quad 1\dfrac{2}{\to}3\quad \dfrac{1}{\to}\,3_4\quad 1\dfrac{4}{\to}5\quad \dfrac{1}{\to}\,5_6\quad \dfrac{6}{\to}7\quad 1\dfrac{}{\to}\,7_8\quad \dfrac{8}{\to}9\quad 1\dfrac{}{\to}\,9_{10}\quad 1\dfrac{10}{\to}11$

$\dfrac{2}{\to}\,2_4\quad 2\dfrac{}{\to}\,3_5\quad \dfrac{2}{\to}\,4_6\quad 2\dfrac{5}{\to}7\quad \dfrac{2}{\to}\,6_8\quad 2\dfrac{7}{\to}9\quad \dfrac{2}{\to}\,8_{10}\quad 2\dfrac{9}{\to}11\quad \dfrac{2}{\to}\,10_{12}$

$\dfrac{3}{\to}\,3_6\quad 3\dfrac{4}{\to}7\quad \dfrac{3}{\to}\,5_8\quad 3\dfrac{6}{\to}9\quad \dfrac{3}{\to}\,7_{10}\quad \dfrac{8}{\to}11\quad 3\dfrac{}{\to}\,9_{12}\quad 3\dfrac{10}{\to}13$

$\dfrac{4}{\to}\,4_8\quad 4\dfrac{5}{\to}9\quad \dfrac{4}{\to}\,6_{10}\quad 4\dfrac{7}{\to}11\quad \dfrac{4}{\to}\,8_{12}\quad 4\dfrac{9}{\to}13\quad \dfrac{4}{\to}\,10_{14}$

$\dfrac{5}{\to}\,5_{10}\quad 5\dfrac{6}{\to}11\qquad\qquad \dfrac{5}{\to}\,9_{14}\quad 5\dfrac{10}{\to}15$

$\dfrac{6}{\to}\,6_{12}\qquad\qquad 6\dfrac{9}{\to}15\quad \dfrac{6}{\to}\,10_{16}$

$7\dfrac{7}{\to}14\qquad \dfrac{7}{\to}\,9_{16}\quad 7\dfrac{10}{\to}17$

$\dfrac{8}{\to}\,8_{16}\quad 8\dfrac{9}{\to}17\quad \dfrac{8}{\to}\,10_{18}$

$\dfrac{9}{\to}\,9_{18}\quad 9\dfrac{10}{\to}19$

Finish $\dfrac{10}{\to}\,10_{20}$

Test Lesson 8

Fact Game 2

Test 8/Extra Practice

a. $10 - \underline{\hspace{1cm}} = \underline{\hspace{1cm}}$

b. $16 - \underline{\hspace{1cm}} = \underline{\hspace{1cm}}$

c. $6 - \underline{\hspace{1cm}} = \underline{\hspace{1cm}}$

d. $8 - \underline{\hspace{1cm}} = \underline{\hspace{1cm}}$

e. $14 - \underline{\hspace{1cm}} = \underline{\hspace{1cm}}$

f. $12 - \underline{\hspace{1cm}} = \underline{\hspace{1cm}}$

g. $4 - \underline{\hspace{1cm}} = \underline{\hspace{1cm}}$

h. $16 - \underline{\hspace{1cm}} = \underline{\hspace{1cm}}$

i. $18 - \underline{\hspace{1cm}} = \underline{\hspace{1cm}}$

j. $14 - \underline{\hspace{1cm}} = \underline{\hspace{1cm}}$

Part 2

a. $9 \times 4 = \underline{\hspace{1cm}}$

b. $10 \times 4 = \underline{\hspace{1cm}}$

c. $6 \times 4 = \underline{\hspace{1cm}}$

d. $5 \times 4 = \underline{\hspace{1cm}}$

e. $8 \times 4 = \underline{\hspace{1cm}}$

f. $7 \times 4 = \underline{\hspace{1cm}}$

g. $4 \times 4 = \underline{\hspace{1cm}}$

h. $4 \times 8 = \underline{\hspace{1cm}}$

i. $4 \times 6 = \underline{\hspace{1cm}}$

j. $4 \times 9 = \underline{\hspace{1cm}}$

Part 3

a. $2 \times \underline{\hspace{1cm}} = 8$

b. $2 \times \underline{\hspace{1cm}} = 18$

c. $1 \times \underline{\hspace{1cm}} = 5$

d. $2 \times \underline{\hspace{1cm}} = 14$

e. $5 \times \underline{\hspace{1cm}} = 25$

f. $2 \times \underline{\hspace{1cm}} = 10$

g. $9 \times \underline{\hspace{1cm}} = 90$

h. $2 \times \underline{\hspace{1cm}} = 16$

i. $2 \times \underline{\hspace{1cm}} = 12$

j. $2 \times \underline{\hspace{1cm}} = 20$

Part 4

a. $1 \underline{\hspace{0.5cm}} \dfrac{4}{5}$

b. $1 \underline{\hspace{0.5cm}} \dfrac{6}{4}$

c. $\dfrac{9}{8} \underline{\hspace{0.5cm}} 1$

d. $\dfrac{7}{7} \underline{\hspace{0.5cm}} 1$

e. $\dfrac{5}{8} \underline{\hspace{0.5cm}} 1$

Part 5

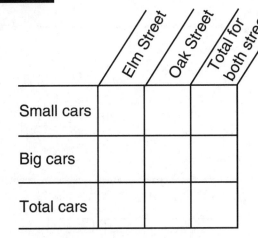

Fact 1: On Elm Street there were 76 cars in all.

Fact 2: The total of all small cars was 49.

Fact 3: On Oak Street there were 20 small cars.

Fact 4: The total of all cars on both streets was 140.

a. Were there more big cars on Elm Street or Oak Street? _____

b. How many big cars were on Oak Street? _____

c. How many total big cars were there? _____

d. Were there more big cars or small cars? _____

e. Were there more cars on Elm Street or on Oak Street? _____

Lesson 81

Part 1

a. 13
    − 7

    $10 - \boxed{} = \underline{}$

c. 11
    − 8
    ▮

    $10 - \boxed{} = \underline{}$

b. 12
    − 5
    ▮

    $10 - \boxed{} = \underline{}$

d. 14
    − 6
    ▮

    $10 - \boxed{} = \underline{}$

Part 2

a. 2⌐‾‾→ 18

d. 3⌐‾‾→ 12

b. 4⌐‾‾→ 20

e. 2⌐‾‾→ 16

c. 2⌐‾‾→ 14

f. 3⌐‾‾→ 15

Part 3 · Independent Work

Complete the sign for each equation.

a. $\dfrac{8}{7}$ __ 1

b. 1 __ $\dfrac{5}{7}$

c. $\dfrac{1}{7}$ __ 1

b. 1 __ $\dfrac{7}{7}$

Part 4 · For each problem, complete the fraction and shade the parts.

a. $\dfrac{5}{}$

b. $\dfrac{4}{}$

c. $\dfrac{4}{}$

d. $\dfrac{1}{}$

Do the independent work for Lesson 81 of your textbook.

Lesson 82

Part 1

a. $13 - 5 =$ _____ $13 - 8 =$ _____   b. $12 - 5 =$ _____ $12 - 7 =$ _____

Part 2

a. $13 - 9 =$ _____   b. $13 - 8 =$ _____   c. $12 - 9 =$ _____   d. $12 - 8 =$ _____

e. $12 - 7 =$ _____   f. $12 - 6 =$ _____   g. $12 - 5 =$ _____   h. $13 - 5 =$ _____

i. $14 - 7 =$ _____   j. $12 - 7 =$ _____   k. $16 - 8 =$ _____   l. $11 - 8 =$ _____

m. $12 - 8 =$ _____   n. $13 - 8 =$ _____

Part 3

a. $5 \overline{\smash{\big)}} 15$ b. $5 \overline{\smash{\big)}} 10$ c. $10 \overline{\smash{\big)}} 60$

d. $7 \overline{\smash{\big)}} 14$ e. $10 \overline{\smash{\big)}} 90$ f. $8 \overline{\smash{\big)}} 16$

Part 4

a. $\dfrac{2 + 3}{5} =$ b. $\dfrac{10 - 7}{3} =$ c. $\dfrac{8 + 9}{10} =$

d. $\dfrac{1 + 3}{5} =$ e. $\dfrac{7 - 5}{5} =$ f. $\dfrac{9 - 3}{8} =$

Part 5

a. $\begin{array}{r} 13 \\ -\ 7 \\ \hline \end{array}$ _____

b. $\begin{array}{r} 14 \\ -\ 8 \\ \hline \end{array}$ _____

c. $\begin{array}{r} 15 \\ -\ 9 \\ \hline \end{array}$ _____

d. $\begin{array}{r} 13 \\ -\ 8 \\ \hline \end{array}$ _____

Lesson 83

Part 1

a. $7 \overline{\smash{\big)}} \longrightarrow 14$ b. $10 \overline{\smash{\big)}} \longrightarrow 40$ c. $5 \overline{\smash{\big)}} \longrightarrow 10$ d. $9 \overline{\smash{\big)}} \longrightarrow 18$

e. $10 \overline{\smash{\big)}} \longrightarrow 90$ f. $6 \overline{\smash{\big)}} \longrightarrow 12$ g. $7 \overline{\smash{\big)}} \longrightarrow 7$

Part 2

a. $\dfrac{5}{3} - \dfrac{2}{3} = \underline{\qquad} = \underline{\quad}$

b. $\dfrac{6}{4} + \dfrac{1}{4} = \underline{\qquad} = \underline{\quad}$

c. $\dfrac{7}{3} - \dfrac{1}{3} = \underline{\qquad} = \underline{\quad}$

d. $\dfrac{6}{4} - \dfrac{5}{4} = \underline{\qquad} = \underline{\quad}$

e. $\dfrac{3}{4} + \dfrac{5}{4} = \underline{\qquad} = \underline{\quad}$

f. $\dfrac{10}{3} - \dfrac{7}{3} = \underline{\qquad} = \underline{\quad}$

g. $\dfrac{12}{5} - \dfrac{8}{5} = \underline{\qquad} = \underline{\quad}$

Part 3

a. $\begin{array}{r} 13 \\ -\ 6 \\ \hline \blacksquare \end{array}$ _____

b. $\begin{array}{r} 15 \\ -\ 8 \\ \hline \blacksquare \end{array}$ _____

c. $\begin{array}{r} 16 \\ -\ 9 \\ \hline \blacksquare \end{array}$ _____

d. $\begin{array}{r} 14 \\ -\ 6 \\ \hline \blacksquare \end{array}$ _____

Part 4

a. $1 \underline{\quad} \dfrac{5}{6}$ b. $1 \underline{\quad} \dfrac{4}{3}$ c. $1 \underline{\quad} \dfrac{7}{7}$ d. $1 \underline{\quad} \dfrac{9}{8}$

e. $1 \underline{\quad} \dfrac{8}{7}$ f. $1 \underline{\quad} \dfrac{7}{8}$ g. $1 \underline{\quad} \dfrac{2}{2}$

Do the independent work for Lesson 83 of your textbook.

Lesson 84

a. $\begin{array}{r} 4\ 7 \\ \times\ 5 \\ \hline \end{array}$

b. $\begin{array}{r} 5\ 3 \\ \times\ 6 \\ \hline \end{array}$

c. $\begin{array}{r} 4\ 3 \\ \times\ 9 \\ \hline \end{array}$

d. $\begin{array}{r} 4\ 5 \\ \times\ 5 \\ \hline \end{array}$

Part 2

a. $7\overline{)}\rightarrow 14$

b. $4\overline{)}\rightarrow 8$

c. $5\overline{)}\rightarrow 15$

d. $5\overline{)}\rightarrow 5$

e. $10\overline{)}\rightarrow 80$

f. $10\overline{)}\rightarrow 20$

g. $2\overline{)}\rightarrow 18$

h. $7\overline{)}\rightarrow 7$

i. $6\overline{)}\rightarrow 12$

j. $2\overline{)}\rightarrow 6$

Part 3

a. $\dfrac{6}{4} + \dfrac{1}{4} = \underline{} = \underline{}$

d. $\dfrac{9}{3} - \dfrac{7}{3} = \underline{} = \underline{}$

b. $\dfrac{8}{5} - \dfrac{1}{5} = \underline{} = \underline{}$

e. $\dfrac{17}{5} - \dfrac{9}{5} = \underline{} = \underline{}$

c. $\dfrac{3}{9} + \dfrac{7}{9} = \underline{} = \underline{}$

Part 4

a. $1 \underline{} \dfrac{7}{6}$

b. $1 \underline{} \dfrac{9}{8}$

c. $1 \underline{} \dfrac{7}{7}$

d. $1 \underline{} \dfrac{8}{9}$

e. $1 \underline{} \dfrac{12}{12}$

f. $1 \underline{} \dfrac{12}{11}$

g. $1 \underline{} \dfrac{11}{10}$

h. $1 \underline{} \dfrac{10}{12}$

Do the independent work for Lesson 84 of your textbook.

Lesson 85

a. 5 2
x 6

b. 6 4
x 6

c. 1 5
x 9

d. 3 4
x 9

e. 9 2
x 5

Part 2

a.

	Street A	Street B	Total for both streets
Red cars	✔	10	
Blue cars	42✔		55
Total cars			95

b.

	Street C	Street D	Total for both streets
Red cars	0	✔	
Blue cars		8✔	28
Total cars	20		

c.

	Street E	Street F	Total for both streets
Red cars		30✔	
Blue cars		✔	40
Total cars	25		75

On Street A <u>there are 12 more blue cars than red cars.</u>

On Street D <u>there are 9 fewer blue cars than red cars.</u>

On Street F <u>there are 10 fewer blue cars than red cars.</u>

Part 3

a. 9 ⟍ 36

b. 9 ⟍ 45

c. 6 ⟍ 12

d. 5 ⟍ 15

e. 4 ⟍ 20

f. 7 ⟍ 28

g. 10 ⟍ 50

h. 7 ⟍ 14

i. 9 ⟍ 18

j. 6 ⟍ 60

Part 4

a. $\dfrac{12}{9} - \dfrac{3}{5} =$ ——— = —

b. $\dfrac{12}{5} - \dfrac{9}{5} =$ ——— = —

c. $\dfrac{5}{2} + \dfrac{7}{2} =$ ——— = —

d. $\dfrac{8}{8} + \dfrac{5}{5} =$ ——— = —

e. $\dfrac{8}{6} - \dfrac{5}{6} =$ ——— = —

f. $\dfrac{10}{9} - \dfrac{9}{9} =$ ——— = —

Lesson 86

a.

	Elm Street	Maple Street	Total for both streets
Yellow cars	17	5	
Brown cars	✔		21
Total cars		24	

On Elm Street <u>there are 15 more yellow cars than brown cars.</u>

b.

	Pine Street	Fir Street	Total for both streets
Yellow cars	12	✔	
Brown cars		39	57
Total cars			90

On Fir Street <u>there are 18 more brown cars than yellow cars.</u>

Part 2

a. $5\overline{)}20$
b. $5\overline{)}15$
c. $10\overline{)}70$
d. $9\overline{)}9$

e. $8\overline{)}16$
f. $4\overline{)}16$
g. $1\overline{)}5$
h. $4\overline{)}20$

i. $5\overline{)}10$
j. $2\overline{)}14$

Part 3

a. ☐
$$\begin{array}{r} 19 \\ \times\ 7 \\ \hline \end{array}$$

b. ☐
$$\begin{array}{r} 24 \\ \times\ 7 \\ \hline \end{array}$$

c. ☐
$$\begin{array}{r} 55 \\ \times\ 9 \\ \hline \end{array}$$

d. ☐
$$\begin{array}{r} 54 \\ \times\ 5 \\ \hline \end{array}$$

Part 4

a. $\dfrac{3}{4} + \dfrac{2}{3} = \underline{\quad} = \underline{\quad}$

b. $\dfrac{3}{10} + \dfrac{9}{10} = \underline{\quad} = \underline{\quad}$

c. $\dfrac{17}{5} - \dfrac{8}{9} = \underline{\quad} = \underline{\quad}$

d. $\dfrac{18}{3} - \dfrac{9}{3} = \underline{\quad} = \underline{\quad}$

e. $\dfrac{12}{4} - \dfrac{7}{7} = \underline{\quad} = \underline{\quad}$

f. $\dfrac{9}{9} + \dfrac{10}{9} = \underline{\quad} = \underline{\quad}$

Lesson 87

a. $1\overline{)6}$ b. $10\overline{)60}$ c. $2\overline{)12}$ d. $7\overline{)14}$

e. $9\overline{)9}$ f. $9\overline{)18}$ g. $4\overline{)20}$ h. $5\overline{)15}$

i. $5\overline{)10}$ j. $10\overline{)80}$

Part 2

a.
$$\begin{array}{r} 95 \\ \times\ 9 \\ \hline \end{array}$$
b.
$$\begin{array}{r} 43 \\ \times\ 5 \\ \hline \end{array}$$
c.
$$\begin{array}{r} 34 \\ \times\ 5 \\ \hline \end{array}$$
d.
$$\begin{array}{r} 35 \\ \times\ 5 \\ \hline \end{array}$$
e.
$$\begin{array}{r} 42 \\ \times\ 7 \\ \hline \end{array}$$
f.
$$\begin{array}{r} 97 \\ \times\ 2 \\ \hline \end{array}$$

Part 3

Work the problems you can work. Draw a line through the problems you cannot work.

a. $\dfrac{7}{2} + \dfrac{10}{2} =$ ——— $= —$ b. $\dfrac{5}{12} + \dfrac{7}{12} =$ ——— $= —$ c. $\dfrac{13}{5} + \dfrac{9}{13} =$ ——— $= —$

Part 4

a.

	A Street	B Street	Total for both streets
Big trees	11 ✔		41
Small trees	✔	20	
Total trees			90

On A Street there are 18 fewer big trees than small trees.

b.

	C Street	D Street	Total for both streets
Big trees		✔	33
Small trees	14	12 ✔	
Total trees	25		

On D Street there are 10 fewer small trees than big trees.

Lesson 88

a. 4 ⟶ 8   f. 4 ⟶ 40

b. 3 ⟶ 12   g. 5 ⟶ 15

c. 2 ⟶ 8   h. 4 ⟶ 16

d. 4 ⟶ 12   i. 2 ⟶ 16

e. 8 ⟶ 32   j. 5 ⟶ 20

Part 3

a. $13 - 6 =$ _____ $13 - 7 =$ _____

b. $14 - 6 =$ _____ $14 - 8 =$ _____

Part 4

a. $\dfrac{13}{2} + \dfrac{1}{2} =$

b. $\dfrac{13}{5} - \dfrac{9}{5} =$

c. $\dfrac{3}{12} + \dfrac{10}{12} =$

d. $\dfrac{15}{10} - \dfrac{6}{10} =$

e. $\dfrac{14}{8} - \dfrac{7}{8} =$

f. $\dfrac{12}{3} - \dfrac{3}{3} =$

Part 2

a.

	Elm Street	Maple Street	Total for both streets
Large trees	11		20
Small trees		6	
Total trees		15	

On Elm Street there are 15 more small trees than large trees.

b.

	Pine Street	Fir Street	Total for both streets
Large trees			30
Small trees		32	
Total trees	50		102

On Fir Street there are 12 more small trees than large trees.

Part 5

a.  50 _____ ⟶ N / C

b.  35 _____ ⟶ N / C

c.  40 _____ ⟶ D / C

d.  20 _____ ⟶ N / C

e.  60 _____ ⟶ D / C

Lesson 89

Part 1

a. 5 ⟌ 8 → ___

b. 5 ⟌ 6 → ___

c. 5 ⟌ 9 → ___

d. 5 ⟌ 7 → ___

Part 3

a. 5 ⟌ → 20

b. 4 ⟌ → 40

c. 2 ⟌ → 14

d. 5 ⟌ → 15

e. 4 ⟌ → 20

f. 3 ⟌ → 12

g. 8 ⟌ → 16

h. 2 ⟌ → 18

i. 7 ⟌ → 14

j. 4 ⟌ → 16

k. 4 ⟌ → 36

Part 2

a.

	Forest	City	Total for both places
Blue birds	70		
Red birds		35	
Total birds		89	200

In the forest there are 29 fewer red birds than blue birds.

b.

	Mountain	Valley	Total for both places
Blue birds	6		
Red birds		13	21
Total birds			50

In the valley there are 10 more blue birds than red birds.

Part 4

a. 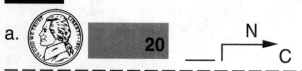 20 → ___ N C

b.  → ___ D C

c. 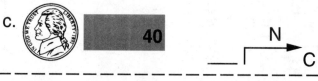 40 → ___ N C

d.  → ___ D C

e.  → ___ N C

134

Lesson 90

a. 5 ⌐9→ ___

b. 5 ⌐6→ ___

c. 5 ⌐8→ ___

d. 5 ⌐7→ ___

Part 2

a. 5 | 20 / 4

b. ☐ | 10 / 2

c. ☐ | 7 / 1

d. ☐ | 50 / 10

e. ☐ | 18 / 2

Part 3

a.

	Forest	City	Total for both places
Blue birds	9		
Red birds		40	61
Total birds			121

In the forest there were 12 fewer blue birds than red birds.

b.

	Forest	City	Total for both places
Yellow birds	12	16	
Green birds			40
Total birds	19		

In the city there were 17 more green birds than yellow birds.

Part 4

a. 4 ⌐=→ 12

b. 4 ⌐=→ 20

c. 4 ⌐=→ 8

d. 4 ⌐=→ 16

e. 4 ⌐=→ 24

f. 4 ⌐=→ 36

Test 9

Part 6 Write the missing small number.

a. 7 ⟶ 28   b. 10 ⟶ 50   c. 5 ⟶ 15   d. 9 ⟶ 45

e. 6 ⟶ 12   f. 9 ⟶ 36   g. 7 ⟶ 14   h. 4 ⟶ 20

Part 7 Write the complete number family for each problem.

a. 20 ___ ⟶ N C

c. 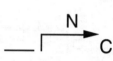 40 ___ ⟶ N C

b. 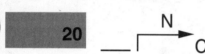 ___ ⟶ D C

d.  ___ ⟶ D C

Part 8 Complete the families.

a. 5 ⟶ 9 ___

b. 5 ⟶ 6 ___

c. 5 ⟶ 8 ___

d. 5 ⟶ 7 ___

Part 9 Fill in all the missing numbers in the table.

	X Street	Y Street	Total for both streets
Red cars		10	
Blue cars	42		128
Total cars			195

On Street X there are 15 fewer blue cars that red cars.

Start

1×1=1	1×2=2	1×3=3	1×4=4	1×5=5	1×6=6	1×7=7	1×8=8	1×9=9	1×10=10

2×2=4	2×3=6	2×4=8	2×5=10	2×6=12	2×7=14	2×8=16	2×9=18	2×10=20

3×4=12 3×5=15 3×9=27 3×10=30

4×4=16 4×5=20 4×6=24 4×7=28 4×8=32 4×9=36 4×10=40

5×5=25 5×9=45 5×10=50

6×9=54 6×10=60

7×9=63 7×10=70

8×9=72 8×10=80

9×9=81 9×10=90

Finish

10×10=100

Test Lesson 9

Fact Game 1

Start

1+1=2 1+2=3 1+3=4 1+4=5 1+5=6 1+6=7 1+7=8 1+8=9 1+9=10 1+10=11

2+2=4 2+3=5 2+4=6 2+5=7 2+6=8 2+7=9 2+8=10 2+9=11 2+10=12

3+3=6 3+4=7 3+5=8 3+6=9 3+7=10 3+8=11 3+9=12 3+10=13

4+4=8 4+5=9 4+6=10 4+7=11 4+8=12 4+9=13 4+10=14

5+5=10 5+6=11 5+7=12 5+8=13 5+9=14 5+10=15

6+6=12 6+7=13 6+8=14 6+9=15 6+10=16

7+7=14 7+8=15 7+9=16 7+10=17

8+8=16 8+9=17 8+10=18

9+9=18 9+10=19

Finish

10+10=20

Test Lesson 9

Fact Game 2

Test 9/Extra Practice

a. 7 ⟶ 14   b. 4 ⟶ 8   c. 5 ⟶ 15   d. 5 ⟶ 5

e. 10 ⟶ 80   f. 10 ⟶ 20   g. 2 ⟶ 18   h. 7 ⟶ 7

i. 6 ⟶ 12   j. 2 ⟶ 6

Part 2

a. 5 —⟶ 8 ____ ____

b. 5 —⟶ 6 ____ ____

c. 5 —⟶ 9 ____ ____

d. 5 —⟶ 7 ____ ____

Part 3

a.

	Forest	City	Total for both places
Blue birds	70		
Red birds		35	
Total birds		89	200

In the forest there are 29 fewer red birds than blue birds.

b.

	Mountain	Valley	Total for both places
Blue birds	6		
Red birds		13	21
Total birds			50

In the valley there are 10 more blue birds than red birds.

Lesson 91

a. 2 4
    x 6

b. 4 9
    x 8

c. 5 9
    x 4

d. 3 6
    x 3

e. 5 4
    x 4

f. 4 2
    x 7

Part 2

	Cars	Trucks	Total vehicles
Elm Street			100
Maple Street			35
Total for both streets		75	

Fact 1: There were 25 cars on Elm Street.

Fact 2: There were 10 more cars on Maple Street than there were on Elm Street.

a. How many cars were on Maple Street? _____

b. How many trucks were there in all? _____

c. Were there more cars or trucks? _____

d. Were there more trucks on Elm Street or on Maple Street? _____

Part 3

a. 4 ⌐→ 16

b. 4 ⌐→ 24

c. 4 ⌐→ 40

d. 4 ⌐→ 32

e. 4 ⌐→ 12

f. 4 ⌐→ 8

Part 4

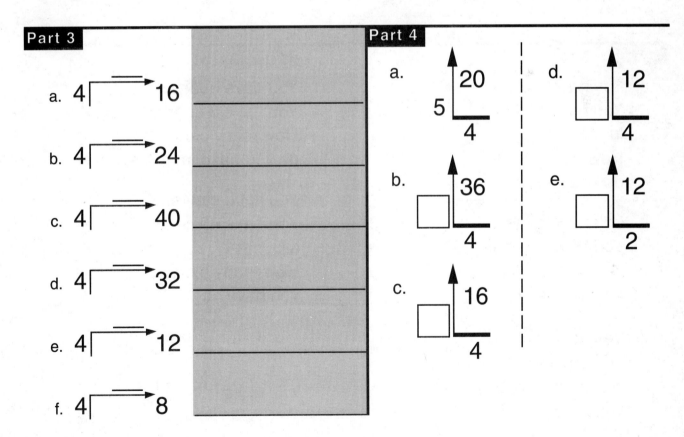

a. 5 | 20 / 4

b. ☐ | 36 / 4

c. ☐ | 16 / 4

d. ☐ | 12 / 4

e. ☐ | 12 / 2

Lesson 92

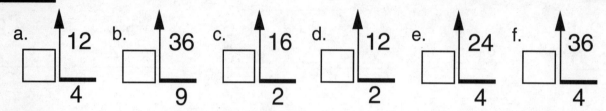

a. 12 4

b. 36 9

c. 16 2

d. 12 2

e. 24 4

f. 36 4

Part 2

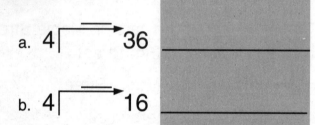

a. 4 ⟶ 36 _____

b. 4 ⟶ 16 _____

c. 4 ⟶ 32 _____

d. 4 ⟶ 24 _____

e. 4 ⟶ 28 _____

f. 4 ⟶ 20 _____

g. 4 ⟶ 12 _____

Part 3

a. You have nickels.
You have 30 cents
in all.
How many nickels
do you have?
____
N ⟶ C

b. You have dimes.
You have 7 dimes.
How many cents do
you have in all?   ____
D ⟶ C

c. You have nickels.
You have 9 nickels.
How many cents do
you have in all?   ____
N ⟶ C

d. You have quarters.
You have 3 quarters.
How many cents
do you have in all? ____
Q ⟶ C

e. You have dimes.
You have 40 cents in
all.
How many dimes do
you have?
____
D ⟶ C

Do the independent work for Lesson 92 of your textbook.

Lesson 93

Part 1

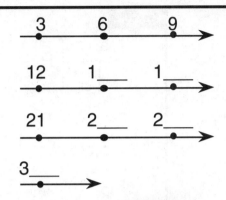

3   6   9

12   1___   1___

21   2___   2___

3___

Part 2

a. 4⌐▔⌐→ 28

b. 2⌐▔⌐→ 12

c. 2⌐▔⌐→ 18

d. 4⌐▔⌐→ 24

e. 5⌐▔⌐→ 20

f. 2⌐▔⌐→ 16

g. 4⌐▔⌐→ 20

h. 5⌐▔⌐→ 15

i. 4⌐▔⌐→ 32

j. 4⌐▔⌐→ 12

k. 4⌐▔⌐→ 36

l. 5⌐▔⌐→ 10

m. 2⌐▔⌐→ 14

n. 4⌐▔⌐→ 28

o. 4⌐▔⌐→ 32

Part 3

a. You have dimes. You have 30 cents in all. How many dimes do you have? _____ ___⌐→ D / C

b. You have nickels. You have 30 cents in all. How many nickels do you have? _____ ___⌐→ N / C

c. You have nickels. You have 8 nickels. How many cents do you have in all? _____ ___⌐→ N / C

d. You have dimes. You have 9 dimes. How many cents do you have in all? _____ ___⌐→ D / C

Part 4

a. 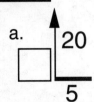 20 / 5

b. 15 / 3

c. 14 / 7

d. 28 / 4

Do the independent work for Lesson 93 of your textbook.

Lesson 94

Part 1

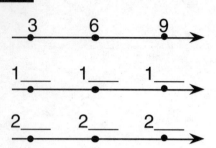

Part 2

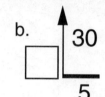

a. 8 / 2

b. 30 / 5

c. 28 / 4

d. 24 / 4

Part 3

a. 2 5 9
   x   4

b. 4 7 2
   x   5

c. 8 9 7
   x   2

d. 4 4 6
   x   4

Part 4

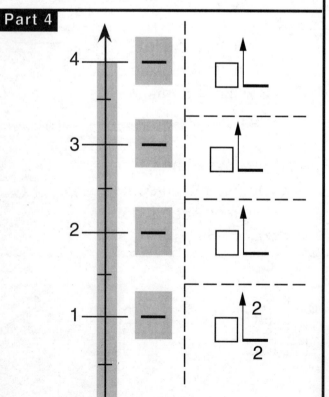

Part 5

a. 9 ⟌ 72

b. 9 ⟌ 54

c. 9 ⟌ 36

d. 9 ⟌ 81

e. 9 ⟌ 27

f. 9 ⟌ 45

g. 9 ⟌ 63

h. 9 ⟌ 18

Do the independent work for Lesson 94 of your textbook.

Lesson 95

Part 1

a. 9⟌→ 45

b. 9⟌→ 36

c. 9⟌→ 63

d. 9⟌→ 27 _____

e. 9⟌→ 72 _____

f. 9⟌→ 54 _____

Part 2

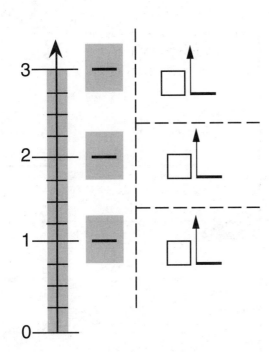

Part 3

a. $\begin{array}{r} 386 \\ \times\ \ \ 4 \\ \hline \end{array}$ b. $\begin{array}{r} 386 \\ \times\ \ \ 2 \\ \hline \end{array}$

c. $\begin{array}{r} 386 \\ \times\ \ \ 5 \\ \hline \end{array}$ d. $\begin{array}{r} 665 \\ \times\ \ \ 9 \\ \hline \end{array}$

Part 4

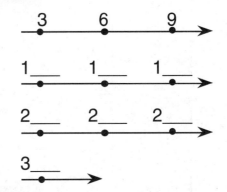

Part 5 — Independent Work

Work each problem.

a. $\begin{array}{r} 42 \\ +\ \ 8 \\ \hline \end{array}$
b. $\begin{array}{r} 56 \\ \times\ 9 \\ \hline \end{array}$
c. $\begin{array}{r} 61 \\ \times\ 9 \\ \hline \end{array}$
d. $\begin{array}{r} 83 \\ -\ 7 \\ \hline \end{array}$
e. $\begin{array}{r} 94 \\ 387 \\ +705 \\ \hline \end{array}$
f. $\begin{array}{r} 107 \\ +\ 93 \\ \hline \end{array}$
g. $\begin{array}{r} 515 \\ -489 \\ \hline \end{array}$

143

Lesson 96

Part 1

a. 9⟌18

b. 9⟌45

c. 9⟌81

d. 9⟌72

e. 9⟌54

f. 9⟌36

Part 2

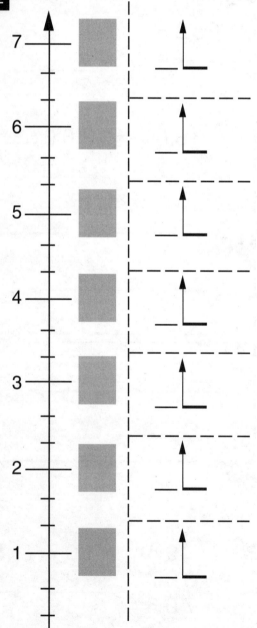

Part 3

a. 937
   x   5

b. 243
   x   9

c. 243
   x   5

d. 243
   x   4

Part 4

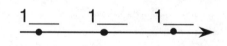

3   6   9

1___   1___   1___

2___   2___   2___

3___

Lesson 97

Part 1

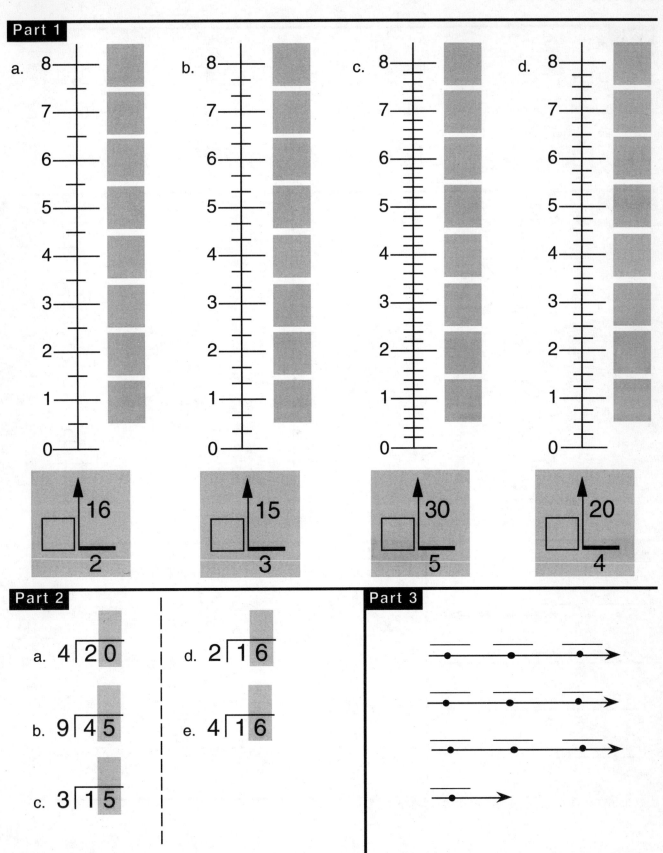

a. [number line 0–8] 16 / 2

b. [number line 0–8] 15 / 3

c. [number line 0–8] 30 / 5

d. [number line 0–8] 20 / 4

Part 2

a. 4)20

b. 9)45

c. 3)15

d. 2)16

e. 4)16

Part 3

Lesson 98

Part 1

a. $5\overline{)4\ 5}$　　b. $2\overline{)1\ 2}$　　c. $4\overline{)2\ 4}$　　d. $2\overline{)1\ 6}$

e. $4\overline{)3\ 6}$　　f. $4\overline{)3\ 2}$　　g. $8\overline{)7\ 2}$

Part 2

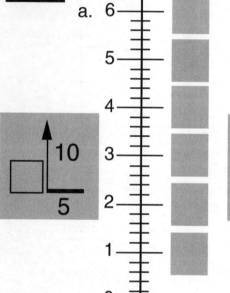

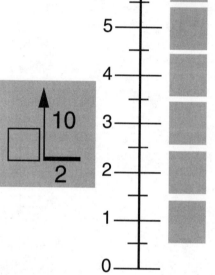

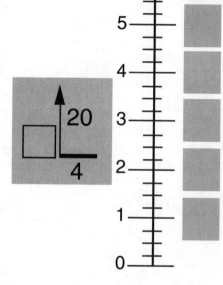

Part 3

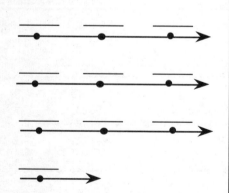

Part 4

a.
$$\begin{array}{r} 984 \\ \times\ \ \ 4 \\ \hline \end{array}$$

b.
$$\begin{array}{r} 689 \\ \times\ \ \ 5 \\ \hline \end{array}$$

c.
$$\begin{array}{r} 182 \\ \times\ \ \ 9 \\ \hline \end{array}$$

d.
$$\begin{array}{r} 789 \\ \times\ \ \ 2 \\ \hline \end{array}$$

e.
$$\begin{array}{r} 456 \\ \times\ \ \ 5 \\ \hline \end{array}$$

Part 5

a.
$$\begin{array}{r} 103 \\ -\ 71 \\ \hline \end{array}$$

b.
$$\begin{array}{r} 76 \\ +67 \\ \hline \end{array}$$

c.
$$\begin{array}{r} 87 \\ -58 \\ \hline \end{array}$$

Lesson 99

a. $10\overline{)3\ 0}$ b. $4\overline{)2\ 0}$ c. $9\overline{)7\ 2}$ d. $3\overline{)1\ 5}$

e. $9\overline{)6\ 3}$ f. $4\overline{)3\ 6}$ g. $6\overline{)5\ 4}$

Part 2

a.

$\square = \dfrac{20}{4}$

b. $\square = \dfrac{45}{5}$ c. $\square = \dfrac{16}{4}$

d. $\square = \dfrac{32}{4}$ e. $\square = \dfrac{14}{7}$

Part 3

a. $\begin{array}{r} 5\ 7 \\ \times\ 5 \\ \hline \end{array}$
b. $\begin{array}{r} 9\ 6 \\ \times\ 5 \\ \hline \end{array}$
c. $\begin{array}{r} 5\ 8 \\ \times\ 4 \\ \hline \end{array}$
d. $\begin{array}{r} 9\ 4 \\ \times\ 9 \\ \hline \end{array}$
e. $\begin{array}{r} 8\ 6 \\ \times\ 4 \\ \hline \end{array}$

Part 4

a. 0 1 2 3 $\dfrac{5}{\square}$

c. $\dfrac{2}{\square}$

b. 0 1 2 3 $\dfrac{3}{\square}$

d. $\dfrac{8}{\square}$

Lesson 100

a. $5\overline{)35}$ b. $9\overline{)81}$ c. $6\overline{)54}$ d. $4\overline{)24}$ e. $4\overline{)32}$ f. $4\overline{)36}$

Part 2

a.

b. $\Box = \dfrac{27}{9}$ c. $\Box = \dfrac{18}{9}$

$\Box = \dfrac{18}{2}$ d. $\Box = \dfrac{10}{5}$ e. $\Box = \dfrac{40}{4}$

Part 3 — Independent Work

Complete the fraction and shade the parts.

a. 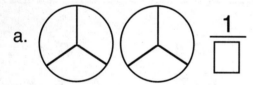 $\dfrac{1}{\Box}$

c. 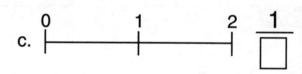 $\dfrac{1}{\Box}$

b. 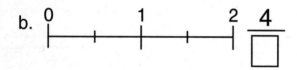 $\dfrac{4}{\Box}$

d.  $\dfrac{8}{\Box}$

Test 10

a. $13 - 7 = $ _____   b. $15 - 7 = $ _____   c. $15 - 8 = $ _____   d. $14 - 6 = $ _____

e. $15 - 9 = $ _____   f. $16 - 7 = $ _____   g. $13 - 8 = $ _____   h. $13 - 5 = $ _____

i. $14 - 8 = $ _____   j. $13 - 9 = $ _____

Part 2

a. $5 \times 6 = $ _____   b. $5 \times 5 = $ _____   c. $8 \times 5 = $ _____   d. $5 \times 7 = $ _____

e. $5 \times 8 = $ _____   f. $6 \times 5 = $ _____   g. $4 \times 5 = $ _____   h. $5 \times 9 = $ _____

i. $5 \times 10 = $ _____   j. $7 \times 5 = $ _____   k. $9 \times 5 = $ _____   l. $3 \times 5 = $ _____

Part 3

a.
$$\begin{array}{r} 937 \\ \times \quad 5 \\ \hline \end{array}$$

b.
$$\begin{array}{r} 243 \\ \times \quad 9 \\ \hline \end{array}$$

Part 4

a. $\square = \dfrac{20}{4}$

b. $\square = \dfrac{27}{9}$

Go to Test 10 in your textbook.

Test 10/Extra Practice

Part 1

a.

b. $\square = \dfrac{27}{9}$

c. $\square = \dfrac{18}{9}$

d. $\square = \dfrac{18}{2}$

e. $\square = \dfrac{10}{5}$

f. $\square = \dfrac{40}{4}$

Lesson 101

Part 1

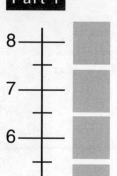

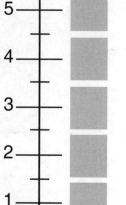

Part 2

a. 1 $\overset{3}{\longrightarrow}$ 3

b. 2 $\overset{3}{\longrightarrow}$ ___

c. 3 $\overset{3}{\longrightarrow}$ ___

d. 3 $\overset{4}{\longrightarrow}$ ___

e. 3 $\overset{5}{\longrightarrow}$ ___

f. 3 $\overset{6}{\longrightarrow}$ ___

Part 3

a. $\square = \dfrac{40}{5}$

b. $\square = \dfrac{18}{9}$

c. $\square = \dfrac{63}{9}$

d. $\square = \dfrac{20}{4}$

e. $\square = \dfrac{20}{2}$

a. $\square = \dfrac{8}{2}$

b. $\square = \dfrac{10}{2}$

c. $\square = \dfrac{12}{2}$

d. $\square = \dfrac{6}{2}$

Part 4

a. 3 $\overset{3}{\longrightarrow}$ ___ _____

b. 3 $\overset{6}{\longrightarrow}$ ___ _____

Lesson 102

Part 1

6 —
5 —
4 —
3 —
2 —
1 —
0 —

a. $\square = \dfrac{12}{3}$ b. $\square = \dfrac{15}{3}$ c. $\square = \dfrac{6}{3}$ d. $\square = \dfrac{3}{3}$

Part 2

a. $3\overline{\smash{)}}\;\overset{3}{\longrightarrow}\;\underline{}$ e. $3\overline{\smash{)}}\;\overset{5}{\longrightarrow}\;\underline{}$ _____

b. $3\overline{\smash{)}}\;\overset{4}{\longrightarrow}\;\underline{}$ f. $3\overline{\smash{)}}\;\overset{3}{\longrightarrow}\;\underline{}$ _____

c. $3\overline{\smash{)}}\;\overset{5}{\longrightarrow}\;\underline{}$ g. $3\overline{\smash{)}}\;\overset{6}{\longrightarrow}\;\underline{}$ _____

d. $3\overline{\smash{)}}\;\overset{6}{\longrightarrow}\;\underline{}$ h. $3\overline{\smash{)}}\;\overset{4}{\longrightarrow}\;\underline{}$ _____

Part 3

a. $5 + 7 = 4 \;\blacksquare\; 3$ b. $3 \times 5 = 18 \;\blacksquare\; 3$ c. $4 \;\blacksquare\; 4 = 8 \times 2$

d. $3 \times 6 = 15 \;\blacksquare\; 3$ e. $10 \;\blacksquare\; 1 = 3 \times 3$ f. $16 - 2 = 7 \;\blacksquare\; 7$

Lesson 103

Part 1

a. $17 \;\blacksquare\; 2 = 5 \times 3$ b. $17 \;\blacksquare\; 3 = 5 \times 4$ c. $2 \;\blacksquare\; 8 = 18 - 2$

d. $20 + 5 = 5 \;\blacksquare\; 5$ e. $20 + 10 = 32 \;\blacksquare\; 2$

a. $\square = \dfrac{24}{4}$ b. $\square = \dfrac{16}{4}$ c. $\square = \dfrac{12}{4}$

d. $\square = \dfrac{32}{4}$ e. $\square = \dfrac{32}{8}$ f. $\square = \dfrac{27}{3}$

Part 3

a. $5\overline{)45}$ b. $5\overline{)25}$ c. $5\overline{)35}$ d. $5\overline{)30}$ e. $5\overline{)40}$

Part 4

a. $3 \times 3 =$ _____   b. $3 \times 6 =$ _____   c. $3 \times 5 =$ _____   d. $3 \times 4 =$ _____

e. $3 \times 2 =$ _____   f. $3 \times 4 =$ _____   g. $3 \times 6 =$ _____   h. $3 \times 5 =$ _____

Part 5

a. $\dfrac{16}{8} = \square$ b. $\dfrac{12}{2} = \square$ c. $\dfrac{16}{2} = \square$

d. $\dfrac{20}{4} = \square$ e. $\dfrac{30}{5} = \square$ f. $\dfrac{10}{5} = \square$

Do the independent work for Lesson 103 of your textbook.

Lesson 104

Part 1

a. $\dfrac{20}{10} = \square$ b. $\dfrac{30}{3} = \square$ c. $\dfrac{30}{30} = \square$ d. $\dfrac{15}{3} = \square$

e. $\dfrac{16}{2} = \square$ f. $\dfrac{14}{2} = \square$ g. $\dfrac{12}{2} = \square$

a. $2 + 8 + 4 = \boxed{} + 4$ b. $6 + 8 + 2 = 17 - \boxed{}$ c. $2 + \boxed{} = 16 - 1 - 1$

d. $\boxed{} \times 2 = 0 + 8$ e. $18 - \boxed{} = 4 \times 4$ f. $\boxed{} + 10 = 14 - 2$

Part 3

a. $5\overline{)30}$ b. $6\overline{)30}$ c. $9\overline{)45}$ d. $5\overline{)35}$

e. $5\overline{)40}$ f. $7\overline{)35}$ g. $8\overline{)40}$

Part 4

a. $6 \times 3 =$ ____   b. $5 \times 3 =$ ____   c. $4 \times 3 =$ ____   d. $3 \times 3 =$ ____

e. $3 \times 5 =$ ____   f. $2 \times 3 =$ ____   g. $1 \times 3 =$ ____   h. $3 \times 6 =$ ____

i. $3 \times 4 =$ ____   j. $3 \times 2 =$ ____   k. $3 \times 6 =$ ____   l. $3 \times 3 =$ ____

Lesson 105

Part 1

a. $3 \times 5 =$ ____   b. $0 \times 3 =$ ____   c. $1 \times 3 =$ ____   d. $6 \times 3 =$ ____

e. $3 \times 4 =$ ____   f. $4 \times 3 =$ ____   g. $5 \times 3 =$ ____   h. $2 \times 3 =$ ____

i. $3 \times 1 =$ ____   j. $3 \times 6 =$ ____   k. $3 \times 0 =$ ____   l. $3 \times 4 =$ ____

Part 2

a. $32 + 3 = 7 \times \boxed{}$ b. $6 \times \boxed{} = 20 - 2$ c. $\boxed{} \times 5 = 10 \times 4$

d. $\boxed{} - 2 = 5 \times 2$ e. $\boxed{} - 1 = 5 \times 4$ f. $\boxed{} \times 3 = 5 - 5$

a. $\dfrac{12}{4} = \square$ b. $\dfrac{15}{3} = \square$ c. $\dfrac{28}{4} = \square$ d. $\dfrac{15}{5} = \square$

e. $\dfrac{32}{4} = \square$ f. $\dfrac{70}{10} = \square$ g. $\dfrac{35}{5} = \square$ h. $\dfrac{10}{10} = \square$

Part 4

a. $9\overline{)45}$ b. $5\overline{)20}$ c. $5\overline{)40}$ d. $5\overline{)45}$

e. $8\overline{)40}$ f. $5\overline{)25}$ g. $6\overline{)30}$

Do the independent work for Lesson 105 of your textbook.

Lesson 106

Part 1

a. $\dfrac{15}{3}$ b. $\dfrac{20}{5}$ c. $\dfrac{30}{6}$ d. $\dfrac{45}{5}$ e. $\dfrac{20}{10}$

Part 2

a. $\dfrac{35}{5} = \square$ b. $\dfrac{50}{5} = \square$ c. $\dfrac{50}{10} = \square$ d. $\dfrac{28}{4} = \square$

e. $\dfrac{30}{5} = \square$ f. $\dfrac{72}{8} = \square$ g. $\dfrac{27}{3} = \square$

Part 3

a. $10\overline{)62}$ P   b. $10\overline{)43}$ P   c. $10\overline{)69}$ P   d. $10\overline{)75}$ P

a. $3\overline{)18}$ b. $3\overline{)12}$ c. $3\overline{)9}$ d. $3\overline{)15}$

e. $3\overline{)12}$ f. $3\overline{)18}$ g. $3\overline{)15}$ h. $3\overline{)9}$

Part 5

a. 8 x 5 = ____ b. 4 x 5 = ____ c. 4 x 4 = ____ d. 4 x 3 = ____

e. 4 x 0 = ____ f. 8 x 0 = ____ g. 8 x 1 = ____ h. 2 x 3 = ____

i. 6 x 3 = ____ j. 5 x 3 = ____ k. 2 x 9 = ____ l. 0 x 3 = ____

Do the independent work for Lesson 106 of your textbook.

Lesson 107

Part 1

a. $3.17   b. $4.42

Part 2

a. 3 →5 ____   e. 3 →3 ____   i. 3 →9 ____

b. 3 →8 ____   f. 3 →6 ____   j. 3 →8 ____

c. 3 →9 ____   g. 3 →4 ____   k. 3 →7 ____

d. 3 →10 ____ h. 3 →7 ____   l. 3 →6 ____

a. 5 ▨ 3 = 12 + 3   b. 17 − 2 = 10 ▨ 5   c. 5 ▨ 5 = 20 + 5

d. ▨ − 7 = 2 x 1   e. 4 x 5 = ▨ x 2   f. 7 ▨ 5 = 30 + 5

Part 4

a. 3⟌12   b. 3⟌18   c. 3⟌15   d. 3⟌9   e. 3⟌6

Part 5

a. $\dfrac{24}{4} = \square$ b. $\dfrac{27}{9} = \square$ c. $\dfrac{18}{9} = \square$ d. $\dfrac{12}{2} = \square$

Part 6

a. 10⟌57
   ⟌ P

b. 10⟌36
   ⟌ P

c. 10⟌81
   ⟌ P

d. 10⟌63
   ⟌ P

e. 10⟌27
   ⟌ P

Do the independent work for Lesson 107 of your textbook.

Lesson 108

Part 1

a. There were 14 gallons in each tank.

b. There were 15 players on each team.

c. Each box held 34 cans.

d. There were 7 lights in each room.

e. The price of each ticket was 4 dollars.

a. $4 \times$ ⬜ $= 30 - 10$ b. ⬜ $- 2 = 4 \times 2$ c. 4 ⬜ $9 = 33 + 3$

d. $8 + 8 = 4$ ⬜ 4 e. $9 \times 7 =$ ⬜ $+ 3$

Part 3

a. $5\overline{)18}$ P   b. $5\overline{)39}$ P   c. $5\overline{)46}$ P   d. $5\overline{)28}$ P

Part 4

a. $4.41   b. $3.93   c. $2.24

Part 5

a. $\begin{array}{r} 3 \\ \times 8 \\ \hline \end{array}$ b. $\begin{array}{r} 3 \\ \times 6 \\ \hline \end{array}$ c. $\begin{array}{r} 3 \\ \times 7 \\ \hline \end{array}$ d. $\begin{array}{r} 3 \\ \times 5 \\ \hline \end{array}$ e. $\begin{array}{r} 3 \\ \times 9 \\ \hline \end{array}$ f. $\begin{array}{r} 3 \\ \times 3 \\ \hline \end{array}$

Do the independent work for Lesson 108 of your textbook.

Lesson 109

Part 1

a. $4\overline{)37}$ R   b. $4\overline{)18}$ R   c. $4\overline{)38}$ R   d. $4\overline{)19}$ R

Part 2

a. $2.86   b. $4.34   c. $1.91

Part 3

a. $\dfrac{35}{5}$ ⌐—

b. $\dfrac{16}{2}$ ⌐—

c. $\dfrac{12}{3}$ ⌐—

d. $\dfrac{45}{5}$ ⌐—

Part 4

a. There were 14 ounces in each bottle.

b. There were 21 miles in each race.

c. Each table had 6 legs.

d. They had 4 meals each day.

Part 5

a. $4\overline{)26}$
    $\underline{24}$ R

b. $2\overline{)13}$
    $\underline{12}$ R

c. $9\overline{)30}$
    $\underline{27}$ R

d. $5\overline{)38}$
    $\underline{35}$ R

e. $3\overline{)23}$
    $\underline{21}$ R

f. $9\overline{)67}$
    $\underline{63}$ R

Part 6

a. 8 x 3 = _____   b. 7 x 3 = _____   c. 9 x 3 = _____   d. 6 x 3 = _____

e. 3 x 5 = _____   f. 3 x 8 = _____   g. 3 x 9 = _____   h. 3 x 7 = _____

i. 7 x 3 = _____   j. 3 x 10 = _____   k. 6 x 3 = _____   l. 8 x 3 = _____

Do the independent work for Lesson 109 of your textbook.

Lesson 110

Part 1

a. $4\overline{)26}$ R

b. $4\overline{)22}$ R

c. $4\overline{)39}$ R

d. $4\overline{)18}$ R

e. $4\overline{)9}$ R

Part 2

a.
```
  9:35
+  :22
  9:57
```

b.
```
  5:16
-  :12
```

c.
```
  6:52
-  :19
```

d.
```
  8:26
+  :19
```

e.
```
  11:24
-   :19
```

f.
```
  6:32
+  :24
```

Part 3

a. $\dfrac{21}{3}$ ⌐

b. $\dfrac{12}{4}$ ⌐

c. $\dfrac{32}{4}$ ⌐

d. $\dfrac{63}{7}$ ⌐

Part 4

a. 24 bugs were in each shed.

b. They put 3 coins in each pocket.

c. 17 girls were in each class.

d. Each bookcase had 9 shelves.

Part 5

a. $3\overline{)20}$ 18 R

b. $9\overline{)59}$ 54 R

c. $5\overline{)36}$ 35 R

d. $9\overline{)40}$ 36 R

e. $4\overline{)37}$ 36 R

f. $2\overline{)15}$ 14 R

Test 11

a. $6\overline{)18}$ b. $4\overline{)12}$ c. $2\overline{)18}$ d. $2\overline{)6}$ e. $9\overline{)45}$ f. $5\overline{)45}$

g. $3\overline{)15}$ h. $4\overline{)24}$ i. $7\overline{)21}$ j. $3\overline{)9}$ k. $4\overline{)16}$

Part 2

a. $5\overline{)20}$ b. $8\overline{)40}$ c. $5\overline{)25}$ d. $6\overline{)30}$ e. $5\overline{)40}$

f. $5\overline{)45}$ g. $4\overline{)20}$ h. $5\overline{)20}$ i. $9\overline{)45}$

Part 3

a. $8 \times 3 =$ _____   b. $4 \times 3 =$ _____   c. $7 \times 3 =$ _____   d. $3 \times 10 =$ _____

e. $3 \times 7 =$ _____   f. $3 \times 9 =$ _____   g. $2 \times 3 =$ _____   h. $3 \times 6 =$ _____

i. $6 \times 3 =$ _____   j. $3 \times 8 =$ _____   k. $9 \times 3 =$ _____

Part 4   Circle the dollars and coins for each problem.

a. $4.41   b. $3.93

Part 5   Work each problem.

a. $5\overline{)36}$ b. $10\overline{)26}$ c. $5\overline{)49}$

$\overline{)}$ R $\overline{)}$ R $\overline{)}$ R

Go to Test 11 in your textbook.

Start

$1\overline{)1}\to 1$ $1\overline{)2}\to 2$ $1\overline{)3}\to 3$ $1\overline{)4}\to 4$ $1\overline{)5}\to 5$ $1\overline{)6}\to 6$ $1\overline{)7}\to 7$ $1\overline{)8}\to 8$ $1\overline{)9}\to 9$ $1\overline{)10}\to 10$

$2\overline{)2}\to 4$ $2\overline{)3}\to 6$ $2\overline{)4}\to 8$ $2\overline{)5}\to 10$ $2\overline{)6}\to 12$ $2\overline{)7}\to 14$ $2\overline{)8}\to 16$ $2\overline{)9}\to 18$ $2\overline{)10}\to 20$

$3\overline{)4}\to 12$ $3\overline{)5}\to 15$ $3\overline{)6}\to 18$ $3\overline{)7}\to 21$ $3\overline{)8}\to 24$ $3\overline{)9}\to 27$ $3\overline{)10}\to 30$

$4\overline{)4}\to 16$ $4\overline{)5}\to 20$ $4\overline{)6}\to 24$ $4\overline{)7}\to 28$ $4\overline{)8}\to 32$ $4\overline{)9}\to 36$ $4\overline{)10}\to 40$

$5\overline{)5}\to 25$ $5\overline{)6}\to 30$ $5\overline{)7}\to 35$ $5\overline{)8}\to 40$ $5\overline{)9}\to 45$ $5\overline{)10}\to 50$

$6\overline{)9}\to 54$ $6\overline{)10}\to 60$

$7\overline{)9}\to 63$ $7\overline{)10}\to 70$

$8\overline{)9}\to 72$ $8\overline{)10}\to 80$

$9\overline{)9}\to 81$ $9\overline{)10}\to 90$

Finish $10\overline{)10}\to 100$

Test Lesson 11

Fact Game

Test 11/Extra Practice

Part 1

a. $9\overline{)45}$ b. $5\overline{)20}$ c. $5\overline{)40}$ d. $5\overline{)45}$

e. $8\overline{)40}$ f. $5\overline{)25}$ g. $6\overline{)30}$

a. $2.86

b. $4.34

c. $1.91

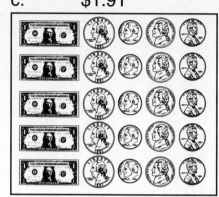

Part 3

a. $4\overline{)26}$
   $\overline{}$ R

b. $4\overline{)22}$
   $\overline{}$ R

c. $4\overline{)39}$
   $\overline{}$ R

d. $4\overline{)18}$
   $\overline{}$ R

e. $4\overline{)9}$
   $\overline{}$ R

Part 4

a. $\dfrac{12}{4} = \square$

b. $\dfrac{15}{3} = \square$

c. $\dfrac{28}{4} = \square$

d. $\dfrac{15}{5} = \square$

e. $\dfrac{32}{4} = \square$

f. $\dfrac{70}{10} = \square$

g. $\dfrac{35}{5} = \square$

h. $\dfrac{10}{10} = \square$

Part 5

a. $5 \;\blacksquare\; 3 = 12 + 3$

b. $17 - 2 = 10 \;\blacksquare\; 5$

c. $5 \;\blacksquare\; 5 = 20 + 5$

d. $\blacksquare - 7 = 2 \times 1$

e. $4 \times 5 = \blacksquare \times 2$

f. $7 \;\blacksquare\; 5 = 30 + 5$

Part 6

a. $\dfrac{21}{3}$ $\overline{}$

b. $\dfrac{12}{4}$ $\overline{}$

c. $\dfrac{32}{4}$ $\overline{}$

d. $\dfrac{63}{7}$ $\overline{}$

Lesson 111

a. 2 ⟌15 ___ R

b. 2 ⟌7 ___ R

c. 4 ⟌25 ___ R

d. 5 ⟌39 ___ R

e. 4 ⟌38 ___ R

f. 2 ⟌19 ___ R

g. 4 ⟌33 ___ R

h. 5 ⟌23 ___ R

Part 2

a. 4:44
  − :36

b. 4:44
  + :13

c. 7:56
  − :29

d. 5:08
  + :37

Part 3

a. 8 x 3 = _____

b. 6 x 3 = _____

c. 7 x 3 = _____

d. 3 x 9 = _____

e. 5 x 3 = _____

f. 8 x 3 = _____

g. 2 x 3 = _____

h. 3 x 6 = _____

i. 3 x 5 = _____

j. 9 x 3 = _____

k. 4 x 3 = _____

l. 3 x 7 = _____

Part 4

	Time the person left	Minutes of trip	Time arrived
Tim	8:25	:30	
Kim		:29	9:35
Slim	7:15		7:41
Jim	8:12	:34	

Lesson 112

Part 1

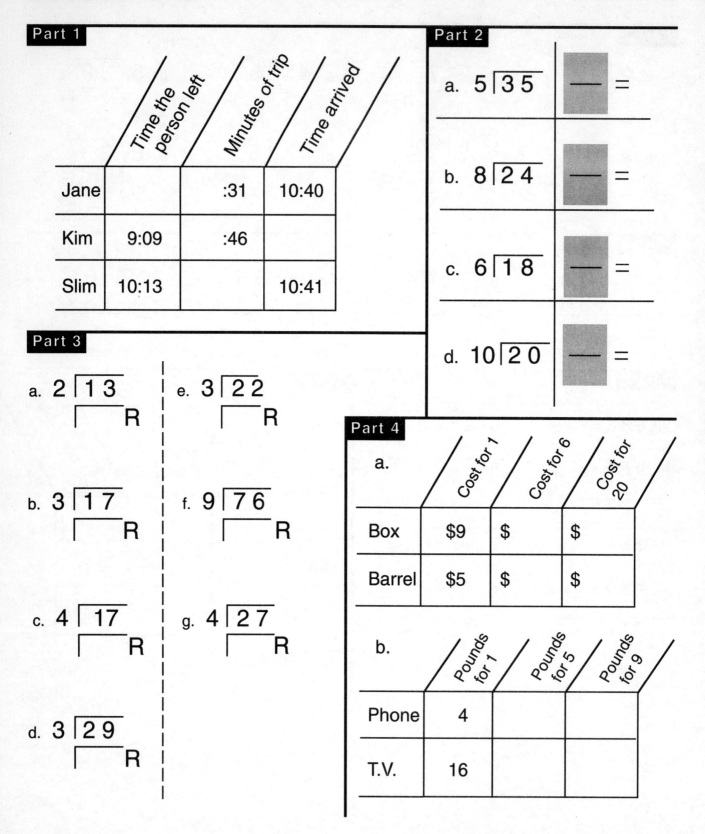

	Time the person left	Minutes of trip	Time arrived
Jane		:31	10:40
Kim	9:09	:46	
Slim	10:13		10:41

Part 2

a. $5\overline{)35}$ ___ =

b. $8\overline{)24}$ ___ =

c. $6\overline{)18}$ ___ =

d. $10\overline{)20}$ ___ =

Part 3

a. $2\overline{)13}$ ___ R

b. $3\overline{)17}$ ___ R

c. $4\overline{)17}$ ___ R

d. $3\overline{)29}$ ___ R

e. $3\overline{)22}$ ___ R

f. $9\overline{)76}$ ___ R

g. $4\overline{)27}$ ___ R

Part 4

a.

	Cost for 1	Cost for 6	Cost for 20
Box	$9	$	$
Barrel	$5	$	$

b.

	Pounds for 1	Pounds for 5	Pounds for 9
Phone	4		
T.V.	16		

Do the independent work for Lesson 112 of your textbook.

Lesson 113

a. $9\overline{)48}$ R

b. $9\overline{)30}$ R

c. $9\overline{)20}$ R

d. $9\overline{)76}$ R

e. $9\overline{)28}$ R

f. $9\overline{)65}$ R

g. $9\overline{)37}$ R

Part 2

	Time the person left	Minutes of trip	Time arrived
Mary	9:11		9:55
Harry		:40	10:59
Barry	7:20	:32	

Part 3

	Cost for 1	Cost for 4	Cost for 9
Drill	$80	$	$
Case of Nails	$20	$	$

Part 4

a. $5\overline{)40}$ — =

b. $\dfrac{18}{3}$ =

c. $\dfrac{54}{9}$ =

d. $4\overline{)32}$ — =

165

Lesson 114

a. $9\overline{)50}$ ___ R   b. $2\overline{)7}$ ___ R   c. $9\overline{)67}$ ___ R   d. $9\overline{)75}$ ___ R

e. $2\overline{)15}$ ___ R   f. $3\overline{)19}$ ___ R   g. $4\overline{)27}$ ___ R

Part 2

a. ___ $\overline{)}$ $\dfrac{24}{4} =$

b. $10\overline{)50}$ — =

c. $9\overline{)63}$ — =

d. ___ $\overline{)}$ $\dfrac{21}{3} =$

Part 3

	Time the person left	Minutes of trip	Time arrived
Ann	2:35	:12	
Fran		:25	4:40
Barry	4:19		4:50

Lesson 115

a. $16 \div 2 =$ ____   b. $24 \div 4 =$ ____   c. $27 \div 9 =$ ____   d. $63 \div 7 =$ ____

Part 2

a. $9 \overline{)65}$ R   b. $9 \overline{)82}$ R   c. $9 \overline{)48}$ R   d. $5 \overline{)48}$ R

e. $2 \overline{)5}$ R   f. $3 \overline{)20}$ R   g. $9 \overline{)59}$ R   h. $4 \overline{)27}$ R

Part 3

	Time the person left	Minutes of trip	Time arrived
a. Kate	8:25	:30	
b. Jim		:20	9:35
c. Slim	9:05		9:40
d. Tim			
e. Kim			

Part 4

a. $2 \times 5 \times 3 =$ _____

b. $3 \times 2 \times 10 =$ _____

c. $2 \times 4 \times 4 =$ _____

d. $2 \times 5 \times 8 =$ _____

e. $2 \times 2 \times 5 =$ _____

f. $3 \times 2 \times 4 =$ _____

d. Tim left at 7:35. The trip took 19 minutes. What time was it when he arrived? _____

e. Kim's trip took 29 minutes. When she arrived, the time was 9:56. What time did she leave? _____

Do the independent work for Lesson 115 of your textbook.   **167**

Lesson 116

a. $4\overline{)28}$ ⌐R   b. $4\overline{)35}$ ⌐R   c. $9\overline{)49}$ ⌐R   d. $3\overline{)11}$ ⌐R

e. $4\overline{)24}$ ⌐R   f. $2\overline{)18}$ ⌐R   g. $4\overline{)23}$ ⌐R   h. $9\overline{)75}$ ⌐R

Part 2

a. $2 \times 4 \times 9 = $ _____

b. $2 \times 5 \times 8 = $ _____

c. $2 \times 4 \times 2 = $ _____

d. $3 \times 3 \times 4 = $ _____

Part 3

a. $15 \div 3 = $ ──── =

b. $30 \div 5 = $ ──── =

c. $16 \div 2 = $ ──── =

d. $18 \div 3 = $ ──── =

e. $10 \div 10 = $ ──── =

f. $18 \div 9 = $ ──── =

Part 4

	Time the person left	Minutes of trip	Time arrived
a. Larry		:17	3:24
b. Harry	2:21		2:40
c. Mary	2:06	:18	
d. Terry			
e. Jerry			

d. Terry's trip to work took 21 minutes. She arrived at 2:23. What time did she leave?

_____

e. Jerry left at 2:13. He arrived at work at 2:30. How long did his trip take? _____

Lesson 117

Part 1

a. $9\overline{)59}$ __ R

b. $5\overline{)30}$ __ R

c. $2\overline{)13}$ __ R

d. $9\overline{)36}$ __ R

e. $4\overline{)28}$ __ R

f. $4\overline{)13}$ __ R

g. $4\overline{)37}$ __ R

h. $9\overline{)30}$ __ R

i. $3\overline{)14}$ __ R

j. $9\overline{)12}$ __ R

Part 2

	Time the person left	Minutes of trip	Time arrived
a. Fran	5:09		5:46
b. Ann		:41	7:56
c. Dan	6:19	:12	
d. Diane			
e. Roxanne			

d. Diane left for the party at 5:15. The trip took 38 minutes. When did she arrive at the party? _____

e. Roxanne left for the party at 5:12. She arrived at 5:31. How long did the trip take? _____

Part 3

a. $21 \div 3 =$ ⬚ $=$

b. $16 \div 2 =$ ⬚ $=$

c. $15 \div 3 =$ ⬚ $=$

d. $25 \div 5 =$ ⬚ $=$

e. $35 \div 7 =$ ⬚ $=$

Do the independent work for Lesson 117 of your textbook.

169

Lesson 118

Part 1

a. $3 \overline{\smash{)}12}$ R

b. $4 \overline{\smash{)}27}$ R

c. $10 \overline{\smash{)}54}$ R

d. $3 \overline{\smash{)}28}$ R

e. $9 \overline{\smash{)}40}$ R

f. $5 \overline{\smash{)}27}$ R

g. $9 \overline{\smash{)}54}$ R

h. $4 \overline{\smash{)}28}$ R

i. $2 \overline{\smash{)}12}$ R

j. $3 \overline{\smash{)}27}$ R

k. $9 \overline{\smash{)}12}$ R

l. $5 \overline{\smash{)}28}$ R

Part 2

a. $3 \overline{\smash{)}27}$

b. $3 \overline{\smash{)}15}$

c. $3 \overline{\smash{)}21}$

d. $3 \overline{\smash{)}18}$

e. $7 \overline{\smash{)}21}$

f. $9 \overline{\smash{)}27}$

g. $3 \overline{\smash{)}9}$

h. $3 \overline{\smash{)}24}$

i. $3 \overline{\smash{)}12}$

j. $8 \overline{\smash{)}24}$

k. $3 \overline{\smash{)}18}$

l. $5 \overline{\smash{)}15}$

Part 3 — Independent Work

Use the information to complete the table.

	Time the person left	Minutes of trip	Time arrived
a. Fran	5:01		5:59
b. Nan			
c. Ann			
d. Dan			

b. Nan's trip took 45 minutes. She left at 12:11. When did she arrive? _____

c. Ann left at 12:12. She arrived at 12:59. How long did her trip take? _____

d. Dan's trip took 49 minutes. He arrived at 1:55. When did he leave? _____

170

Lesson 119

a. $3\overline{)21}$ b. $2\overline{)12}$ c. $3\overline{)27}$ d. $5\overline{)15}$

e. $3\overline{)12}$ f. $6\overline{)24}$ g. $3\overline{)24}$ h. $3\overline{)18}$

i. $9\overline{)27}$ j. $7\overline{)21}$ k. $3\overline{)18}$ l. $6\overline{)24}$

Part 2

a.

	Dollars for 1	Dollars for 9
Box	$	$72
Board	$	$45
Sack	$	$18

b.

	Dollars for 1	Dollars for 4
Box	$	$24
Carton	$	$36
Basket	$	$20

Part 3 — Independent Work

	Time the person left	Minutes of trip	Time arrived
a. Kate	8:25	:30	
b. Jim		:20	9:35
c. Slim	9:05		9:40
d. Tim			
e. Kim			

d. Tim left at 7:35. The trip took 19 minutes. What time was it when he arrived? _____

e. Kim's trip took 29 minutes. When she arrived the time was 9:56. What time did she leave? _____

Test 12

Part 1

a. _____   b. _____   c. _____

Part 2

a. 3 ⟌ 2 1   b. 3 ⟌ 1 5   c. 3 ⟌ 2 4   d. 3 ⟌ 9

e. 3 ⟌ 2 7   f. 3 ⟌ 1 2   g. 3 ⟌ 6   h. 3 ⟌ 1 8

Part 3 Write the number family and figure out the answer.

a. 5 inches of rain fell each day. 45 inches of rain fell. How many days did it rain?

b. There were 25 birds in each tree. There were 9 trees. How many birds were there in all?

Part 4 Write the multiplication problem and the answer for each problem. Remember the units.

a.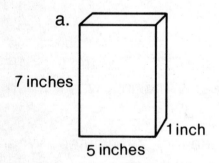

7 inches

5 inches

1 inch

b.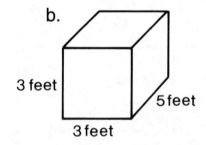

3 feet

3 feet

5 feet

Go to Test 12 in your textbook.

Test 12/Extra Practice

		Time the person left	Minutes of trip	Time arrived
a.	Kate	8:25	:30	
b.	Jim		:20	9:35
c.	Slim	9:05		9:40
d.	Tim			
e.	Kim			

d. Tim left at 7:35. The trip took 19 minutes. What time was it when he arrived? _____

e. Kim's trip took 29 minutes. When she arrived the time was 9:56. What time did she leave? _____

a. 10 + 4 = 14   b. 10 + 7 = 17   c. 9 + 5 = 14
d. 9 + 7 = 16   e. 9 + 3 = 12   f. 10 + 3 = 13
g. 9 + 9 = 18   h. 2 + 9 = 11   i. 5 + 9 = 14
j. 8 + 9 = 17   k. 2 + 10 = 12   l. 7 + 10 = 17
m. 6 + 9 = 15   n. 10 + 9 = 19

Lesson 17, part 4

$$
\begin{array}{cccc}
\text{a.} & 3\,\overset{4}{\cancel{5}}{}^{1}6 & \text{b.} & 3\;7\;7 \\
& -2\;4\;9 & & -1\;2\;7 \\
\hline
& 1\;0\;7 & & 2\;5\;0
\end{array}
$$

$$
\begin{array}{cccc}
\text{c.} & 3\,\overset{3}{\cancel{4}}{}^{1}7 & \text{d.} & 9\,\overset{6}{\cancel{7}}{}^{1}0 \\
& -2\;2\;8 & & -7\;6\;1 \\
\hline
& 1\;1\;9 & & 2\;0\;9
\end{array}
$$

Lesson 18, part 3

a. 4 + 4 = 8   b. 4 + 5 = 9   c. 4 + 8 = 12   d. 4 + 9 = 13
e. 4 + 10 = 14   f. 4 + 2 = 6   g. 4 + 7 = 11   h. 4 + 1 = 5
i. 4 + 6 = 10   j. 4 + 9 = 13   k. 4 + 4 = 8   l. 4 + 3 = 7

Lesson 112, part 2   **Paired Practice Answer Key**

a. 8 x 3 = 24   b. 3 x 3 = 9   c. 2 x 3 = 6   d. 3 x 6 = 18
e. 10 x 3 = 30   f. 3 x 7 = 21   g. 7 x 3 = 21   h. 9 x 3 = 27
i. 3 x 8 = 24   j. 5 x 3 = 15   k. 3 x 4 = 12   l. 3 x 10 = 30
m. 6 x 3 = 18   n. 3 x 5 = 15   o. 4 x 3 = 12   p. 3 x 9 = 27
q. 3 x 3 = 9

Lesson 119, part 4   **Paired Practice Answer Key**

a. 3) 24 = 8   b. 4) 24 = 6   c. 8) 24 = 3   d. 5) 25 = 5
e. 3) 18 = 6   f. 3) 27 = 9   g. 4) 28 = 7   h. 7) 35 = 5
i. 4) 36 = 9   j. 4) 32 = 8   k. 4) 20 = 5   l. 9) 81 = 9
m. 9) 54 = 6   n. 9) 45 = 5   o. 9) 18 = 2   p. 9) 27 = 3

Lesson 120, part 4   **Paired Practice Answer Key**

a. 9) 72 = 8   b. 4) 28 = 7   c. 4) 16 = 4   d. 4) 8 = 2
e. 10) 40 = 4   f. 7) 21 = 3   g. 4) 24 = 6   h. 6) 30 = 5
i. 9) 27 = 3   j. 9) 36 = 4   k. 8) 32 = 4   l. 3) 27 = 9
m. 3) 21 = 7   n. 3) 24 = 8   o. 3) 18 = 6